# On the Fly

# On the Fly

## Executing Strategy in a Changing World

## Stephen J. Wall

**WILEY**

John Wiley & Sons, Inc.

*For Margaret M. Wall—always so proud*

*To make plans and project designs brings with it many good sensations, and whoever had the strength to be nothing but a forger of plans his whole life long would be a very happy man; but he would occasionally have to take a rest from this activity by carrying out a plan—and then comes the vexation and the sobering up.*

—Friedrich Nietzsche, *Assorted Opinions and Maxims*, No. 85

# Contents

# Preface

*As architectural plans for fortifications became increasingly complex, the time it took to build them increased as well, and with it the probability that as soon as they were finished, if not before, they would have been overtaken by further developments, both in artillery and strategic planning, which took account of the growing realization that everything was decided in movement, not in a state of rest.*

—W.G. Sebald[1]

Confronted with continuous upheavals in their environment, many people in the business world have become skeptical about companies' ability to formulate meaningful plans for their future. In the current climate, they argue, when adapting swiftly to change is all-important, strategic planning just will not work: It is a vestige of the past, when the world you were operating in was stable, when transformation happened at a leisurely pace that the company's strategists could absorb in time for the *next* plan.

Yet the fact remains that, in order to operate effectively, organizations still require a clear sense of their direction and a vision of what they will be doing in the future. They must have a way of figuring out how they will be different from their competitors, and what courses of action they are capable of pursuing effectively. In fact, as I argue in this book, in order to retain their identity in a constantly changing world, organizations need strategic focus more than they ever did. What they have to rid themselves of is the notion that what they are doing now or did in the past will work in the future. How then, can they formulate and implement strategies in ways that allow them to adapt rapidly to change without losing their focus and sense of identity?

The choice between traditional strategic planning, with its emphasis on analysis and control, and the kind of flexibility that allows for timely responsiveness, is too often presented as an either/or proposition. It is like a lot of the other choices businesses face: They assume that they have to aim for either efficiency of production *or* the ability to customize products to customers' needs. They believe that they can encourage either discipline *or* creativity. They try to decide whether to increase revenues *or* contain costs. Sometimes this tendency is further exaggerated by oppositional attitudes in the organization itself. People feel they have to fight for their point of view, that someone always has to win and someone else has to lose. They are so busy fighting for their points of view that they cease to listen to each other.

Couching the decisions that businesses have to make in such starkly oppositional, black-and-white terms does not allow for choices that go beyond either/or, A-or-B thinking to get to Point C. The same is true of the debate over strategy: Instead of choosing between a clear sense of direction and differentiation and the ability to adapt to change, ask yourself, How can we plan for responsiveness? How can we formulate and implement strategies in a way that implicitly acknowledges and prepares us for continuing change in the future, as well as taking our internal strengths and weaknesses into account? What kinds of strategies are in and of themselves adaptive?

When you look at your business's strategies in these more inclusive terms, you will still need to make choices, but they will be different ones, involving putting things together in new ways. Often, approaches that look oppositional in the abstract are not so oppositional in reality; all sorts of intriguing combinations are possible, depending on the situation. What you really need to decide is how to come up with the best combination, how to take the most useful elements of each approach and arrive at a coherent plan of action. (Coherence is not necessarily synonymous with simplicity.) That can be achieved only when people *do* listen to each other, when they have learned to look at strategy as an ongoing process of dialogue and adaptation.

The same principles apply to both strategy itself and the means by which it is arrived at. Here, too, the choices have been represented as either/or decisions: Either we will have designated strategic planners who engage in a formal process, *or* we will allow strategies to evolve as the marketplace dictates. Either we will establish a clear strategic focus that will determine people's actions, *or* we will let individuals pursue whatever avenues look promising.

In my work as a managing vice president of Right Management Consultants, a global human resources consulting firm that has worked with 80 percent of the Fortune 500 companies, I have found that success often involves combining the most beneficial elements of two different choices in order to come up with a third option. As I see it, one of the most useful things I can do for my clients—executives and managers in such companies as

UBS, GE, PolyOne, the New York Stock Exchange, MetLife, Intercontinental Hotels, Eaton, and Dyno Nobel—is to work with them to arrive at innovative solutions that go outside the either/or categories. Such solutions were vital to the success of UBS' acquisition of PaineWebber, and to the Dyno Nobel merger with The Ensign-Bickford Company, which will create the largest industrial explosives company in the world. When I consider the difference between strategy as it is taught in the classroom and strategy as it is played out in the real world, I am convinced that the kinds of inclusive choices we offer our clients, and that are presented in this book, are the best possible way to prosper in times of upheaval.

In 1995 I co-authored *The New Strategists*, a book on strategic planning that emphasizes the need to allow strategies to evolve in response to external changes. It also addresses the importance of involving people at all levels of the organization in strategic decision making. In *On the Fly*, I expand on the ideas in that book to offer a more radical model of strategy making that allows for rapid, effective responses to the ever-increasing rate of change while also making use of the creative energies of all an organization's employees.

Since *The New Strategists* was published, more and more companies in a diverse range of industries have recognized that the insights and front-line knowledge of their employees constitute a key source of differential advantage. Drawing on examples from a broad range of businesses, industries, and strategic states, *On the Fly* describes a wide variety of innovative approaches and programs that organizations have employed to help them meet their customers' needs. At the same time, it proposes guidelines for encouraging creativity while containing risk, and for maintaining strategic focus and coherence while still allowing for maximum adaptiveness and flexibility.

It is never possible, of course, to find an all-inclusive solution, and any choice necessarily involves a "road not taken."
Once you accept, however, that there is no single magic para-
digm that enables people to arrive at the perfect strategy, you are
faced with the question: How can I use the different paradigms
available to come up with an effective plan of action for my particular company? How can I customize not just my strategy but
also the process by which that strategy is arrived at, to find the
best approach for my business?

The working model for this book is that you do not have to
sacrifice all the potential benefits of one approach to strategy in order to go with another. *On the Fly* does not propose a single, one-
size-fits-all formula for successful strategy making. Instead, while
emphasizing the role of people at all levels of the organization, it
offers a way of resolving the strategy dilemma and finding the optimum mix of strategic activities for your particular business—one
that will allow it to thrive and grow in these turbulent times.

# I

# Creating a Strategy-Making Organization

# 1 | A New Approach to Strategy

Whether consciously or not, your company is already adhering to one theory of strategy or another. What it may not have done is to tailor its approach to strategic questions to its own needs and priorities. Instead, it could be acting on unexamined assumptions about what its strategy should be and how it should be arrived at. Sometimes, those unexamined assumptions can limit a business's ability to shape its future, or even place that future in jeopardy.

As I note in the Preface to this book, issues relating to strategy are too often viewed as either/or dichotomies: Businesspeople think, for instance, that they have to choose between meeting current market needs and attempting to predict future ones, or between deliberate planning and allowing strategies to emerge. In fact, the ultimate goal is not to choose a single approach to strategy but to strike exactly the right balance for your specific company and situation. Such a balance will enable a business to maintain a coherent sense of direction while also being adaptive and flexible enough to respond fluidly and quickly to the turbulent conditions in its

3

environment. Balance will allow your business to reap the benefits of rational planning processes while still achieving maximum responsiveness to customers.

What is required are systems and structures that are both dynamic enough to respond to new information from the outside and influence the environment they operate in, and fluid enough to accommodate a good deal of disorder without lapsing into real chaos. As such leading management theorists as James Brian Quinn, Robert G. Eccles, Nitin Nohria, and Tom Peterson have argued, the optimal state for an organization is one of "functional chaos." One of the key questions I seek to answer in this book is what such a state would look like in terms of strategy.

Essentially, there are two main debates concerning strategy: strategic fit versus strategic foresight, and deliberate planning versus allowing strategies to emerge. While these debates may be more explicitly aired in business school classrooms than in the halls of corporations, they are actually played out in real-world situations. Let us begin by examining the arguments from both sides.

*Strategic fit versus foresight.* According to one school of thought, the success of a strategy will depend on its degree of strategic fit, that is, the alignment between what the customer wants and the strengths of the organization. Adherents of this view believe in thoroughly researching customer needs, analyzing internal capabilities, and then coming up with product–service offerings directly based on their findings.

Proponents of foresight, on the other hand, argue that the best you can hope for if you aim for strategic fit is a me-too, catch-up strategy with a built-in blindness to change. Do not focus on what customers want now, they say; try to anticipate what they will want tomorrow. Your job is to identify customer needs before customers themselves are aware of them, and identify markets that have not yet been recognized. Do not just analyze: Dare to prophesize. After all, that is what successful companies like Starbucks, The Body Shop, MTV, and CNN all did: They created new markets by foreseeing what customers would want if only they could have it.

*Deliberate planning versus allowing strategies to emerge.* This debate centers on how strategy should be formulated and who should be involved. The argument for deliberate planning is threefold: (1) A methodical planning process is the only way to make sure that all relevant factors will be taken into account. (2) Senior managers are better equipped to carry out the planning process than anyone else; not only do they have the broadest perspective on the organization's resources and goals, and the environment in which it operates, they also have access to all different types of data. (3) Employees need a clear statement of strategy and a plan document to provide them with focus and direction.

Opponents of this more traditional approach argue, however, that today's rapidly changing business climate makes such a linear process outmoded; in fact, it may even be dangerous, since it does not allow for new information to be absorbed and acted on quickly. Arguing that strategy is best arrived at by fluid processes of continual adaptation to the environment, they maintain that lower-level people in direct contact with customers need to participate in the process, or the organization's strategy will not accurately reflect the realities of the marketplace. (This less traditional process of arriving at strategy has come to be known as "strategy making.")

Adherents of more formal planning are skeptical of this argument: As they see it, allowing strategy to evolve in response to the environment, and getting more people involved in making it, result in a loss of focus. A company that is always scrambling to respond to external factors cannot maintain its sense of direction, and having everyone empowered to make decisions about strategy means that nobody knows who is in charge. That can paralyze rather than energize people.

## The Strategic Dilemma

So those are the choices as they are traditionally laid out. Either base your strategy on the fit between your organization's strengths and weaknesses and the current demands of the marketplace, *or* try to anticipate what customers will want—or *would* want if someone were smart enough to offer it—a year from now. Either arrive at your strategy through a formal planning process, conducted by senior management, *or* allow strategy to emerge though a more participative, fluid process, involving as many people as possible. Either regard strategy as a fixed plan of action that gives the organization focus, *or* think of it as something adaptive and flexible.

That all seems pretty clear, doesn't it? But why does strategy making have to be an either/or proposition? What if there were a third alternative, a synthesis that combined the benefits of each approach?

Let us begin by looking at what those benefits are.

### Strategic Fit

There is no doubt that strategies based on the alignment of internal strengths and external needs have historically proved very profitable. Using research and analysis to figure out what the market demands—and how much it will want—and then determining what the company needs to do in order to fill that demand gets rid of some of the uncertainties surrounding strategy formulation. Even if there is no such thing as a surefire strategy, an accurate picture of what is required to meet a market demand

and/or gain a unique competitive advantage—Market and customer reach? Technology leadership? Service differentiation?—allows you to address deficits before they lead to problems. It can also prevent an organization from entering a business or market at which it just is not equipped to succeed.

For example, when diversification was the rage, back in the 1970s, organizations could have benefited from understanding the concept of strategic fit. Because they tried to enter businesses that they knew nothing about, or to succeed in markets that they lacked the competencies to service, many of them wound up with disasters on their hands.

### Strategic Foresight

Strategic foresight, as its name suggests, is a matter of envisioning what customers will want and need in the future, and what will be required for delivery. Sometimes it entails the ability to imagine not only the kind of change that is continuous with the

---

A good example of strategic fit was the Fiat Punto. Fiat invited potential customers to visit their web site and indicate which of many possible features—all of which Fiat was well equipped to provide—were important to them. More than 3,000 people took them up on this invitation. As a result, Fiat was able to design a car that accurately reflected its customers' needs and priorities.[1] Other companies, like Cisco Systems, have used their web sites to enable customers to cocreate features for the products they purchase, a policy that has helped Cisco to increase revenues while simultaneously reducing installation costs.[2]

present, but also radical, discontinuous change. In its most visionary form, strategic foresight can mean foreseeing dramatic changes in the entire industry in which the organization competes, or even the creation of a whole new industry.

For example, the government has recently announced that it will subsidize U.S. auto makers' efforts to develop environmentally friendly, fuel-cell-powered vehicles. Currently, the technology is prohibitively expensive, and there is no method of distributing the hydrogen that fuel cells need. However, if this changes, what will happen to the automobile industry and all the industries dependent on it? What is going to happen to oil companies if cars are no longer powered by gas? What new kinds of industries will spring up? There are a lot of people out there giving those questions serious thought right now.

The most dramatic examples of strategic foresight are those that involved creating whole new products or new markets. The first Polaroid camera, the Sony Walkman, and Apple Computer's introduction of the computer into nonwork settings are all classic examples. The handheld computer is another case in point. A new product created a new market by tapping into an unrecognized need. No one could be sure the need existed until the means were there to satisfy it; intuition, a hunch about what people might want, played an important part.

Yet strategic foresight can also involve not product or market innovations per se, but determining what types of internal resources and skills an organization is likely to need in order to come up with cutting-edge products and deliver them to the marketplace in a competitive fashion. Gary Hamel and C.K. Prahalad, two of the leading writers on the subject, insist that "competing for the future" is essentially a matter of ensuring that the core competencies are in place to exploit the unknown opportunities that will arise and satisfy customer requirements.[3]

This slightly less dramatic type of strategic foresight is more clearly linked to analytical and planning processes, although predicting what competencies will be required in the industry of the future may require as much vision and inspiration as coming up with a whole new type of product.

Sometimes strategic foresight can take the form of investing in the future even when that future looks uncertain. For example, companies that embark on education programs or initiatives to improve business processes during a period of recession find themselves in a better position to take advantage of the recovery when it comes. Texas Instruments' decision to invest in an ambitious effort to come up with a single-chip cell phone at a time when chip sales had experienced their worst decline ever is another such example of foresight—or will be if it pans out. So is Lehman Brothers' refusal to lay off employees in the market downturn of late 2002, when almost all the other big financial firms were downsizing. When the upturn comes, Lehman Brothers' full complement of employees (with years of experience) will be in place to take advantage of it.

## Formal Strategic Planning

A crucial benefit of the formal planning process is its built-in guarantee that things *will not* just happen; it ensures that control will be exerted, to help the organization retain its strategic focus. By forcing the organization to analyze and identify its strengths and weaknesses, its core competencies, the threats that it faces and the opportunities it is qualified to exploit, formal strategic planning strengthens its understanding of who it is and what it is equipped to accomplish.

Plans made on an ad hoc basis by people within a particular function or business unit will inevitably reflect the concerns of those people and that business. When senior managers formulate strategy, however, they are more likely to be objective and to see the larger picture. They also have more facts at their disposal, and can gather information from all areas of the organization. Because they have the tools and the training to sift through data; because they can interpret it, weigh up its relative importance, and arrive at decisions based on a systematic assessment, senior managers are uniquely qualified to evaluate various strategies' likelihood of success.

Another advantage of a deliberate, linear process is that it allows the organization to arrive at a clear definition of where it wants to go, how it plans to get there, and how it can measure its progress toward the goal. Thinking through how you can differentiate yourselves, how you can win, what you are uniquely qualified to do—and what you do not want to do—can only be beneficial to the company as it goes forward.

Who would choose to set out on a journey without a map? You cannot get to where you are going if you do not know where it is. The formal plan is a kind of road map to be consulted along the way. Finally, even in a turbulent world, having such a road map will provide a context for dealing with the unexpected as it arises. In order to respond effectively to change, companies need a clear sense of their capabilities and the kinds of resources they can draw on when they are required to adapt to changing circumstances.

### Allowing Strategies to Emerge

Reacting to what is actually happening now, rather than basing your actions on what happened in the past or might happen in the future, allows an organization to recognize opportunities in unexpected places or in unexpected forms—or to recognize that something no one had mandated is actually in the process of happening anyway.

Unlike the type of deliberate strategy that results from a formal, highly rational planning process, strategy that emerges organically may have its basis in intuition and flashes of insight (like strategic foresight). That could be one of its strengths. As the strategy theorist Henry Mintzberg has pointed out, the "hard information" that senior people rely on when formulating plans is "often limited in scope, lacking richness and often failing to encompass important noneconomic and nonquantitative factors. Much information important for strategy-making never does become hard fact. The expression on a customer's face, the mood in the factory, the tone of voice of a government official. . . .": These cannot be reduced to data on a page.[4]

In fact, strategies have always emerged rather than being exclusively mandated from above. Sometimes they have even been born out of accidents. The classic historical example of this is Scotchgard, which had its inception in an accident in a lab: One of the lab assistants accidentally dropped a bottle that contained a batch of synthetic latex, and some of it spilled on his canvas tennis shoes. Everybody tried to rinse it off, but each thing they used ran off the shoes like water off a duck's back. It was very annoying at the time—but it inspired a very profitable product.

In other cases, strategy has evolved out of an unintended consequence of a deliberate strategy. When the CEO of American Express had trouble cashing a check, he resorted to traveler's checks, and realized how to make money on the float. Similarly, an AmEx employee in Paris started giving travel advice and helping people to book trains and boats when they came in to buy checks. Though at first he was asked not to do this, it proved so lucrative that it was finally adopted as a deliberate strategy.

While AmEx's CEO was the first to recognize the potential of the traveler's check, it is often the people on the front lines who spot opportunities first. A closeness to customers on a daily basis makes such employees uniquely qualified to recognize changes as they occur. The idea for Starbucks' blended coffee drink, Frappuccino, for example, came from the field. Although Howard Schultz, the company's founder and chairman, was doubtful that the new drink would take off, he was outnumbered by other managers, and Frappuccino turned out to be one of Starbucks' most successful product launches.

Other examples of spotting and creating business opportunities include: (1) the baggage handler at British Airways who came up with a way to expedite the handling of first-class baggage, which enabled the carrier to improve its relations with its most profitable customers and gave it a new marketing tactic;[5] (2) the two low-level employees who used the thread they were developing for astronauts' space suits to floss their teeth, thus giving birth to Glide dental floss; (3) the finance and accounting department employee of Mail Boxes Etc, whose memo to CEO Jim Amos convinced him to enter the lucrative business of offering a broad range of technical services to the home office market.[6]

By its very nature, and because it relies on the insights of people at all levels of the organization (or even outside it), allowing strategy to emerge is directly linked to a more freewheeling, participative culture; at the same time, it helps to build such a culture. The one thing it cannot do is to succeed in a rigidly hierarchical organization.

## Combining Fit and Foresight: Why You Need Both

Some of the great business success stories of our time are tales of strategic foresight. Who would not choose to tap into the kind of vast unidentified market that Steve Jobs and Steve Wozniak discovered—or created—for the personal computer?

Yet given the importance of timing in achieving competitive advantage, foresight can sometimes mean hitting on a brilliant idea whose time has not yet come. The English inventor Ian Sinclair, for example, came up with the idea of the personal computer long before Jobs and Wozniak . . . in fact, long before the market was ready for it. Because he had a plan for the future, but none for the present, he found himself in the position of offering the world what it was *going* to need, but not what it wanted right at that time. The same was true of Studebaker, when they introduced the minivan 15 years before anyone else. They had recognized an untapped need, but unfortunately customers remained oblivious to that need for more than a decade. Studebaker's foresight, like Sinclair's, led not to competitive advantage, but to business failure.

All too often, companies that attempt to create demand from an undefined market fall flat on their faces. Coming out with the right product at the wrong time can be as disastrous as failing to come out with the wrong product. Even Apple, when it introduced its now-defunct Newton, was guilty, as one commentator said, of "delivering products ahead of their time."[7] It was the upstart Palm Pilot, which came along three years later, that wound up dominating the market that Newton had opened up.

Moreover, sometimes customers think they want something, only to discover they really don't. For instance, when Web Van offered to do people's grocery shopping for them, a lot of consumers thought it would be great not to have to go to the supermarket any more. They signed up for the service, tried it once, and realized that not only was it impossible to pick out produce over the Web, but they actually *liked* shopping; they liked going in with their list of 8 necessary items and coming out with 20 more they hadn't planned to buy. First-time Web Van customers were plentiful; return customers were practically nonexistent.

Much of what is involved is not merely foresight but luck—and counting on being lucky is too big a gamble for any organization to afford. Yet in today's volatile climate, depending on a fit between organizational strengths and the current demands of the marketplace may be equally dangerous. After all, the very concept of strategic fit rules out the possibility of creating new markets, of imagining something that does not exist yet. It is also based on an unspoken assumption that the future will be a continuation of the past, which is extremely unlikely.

That's why organizations need to combine foresight on the one hand and strategic fit on the other: They need to serve customers' current needs as efficiently and effectively as possible *while also thinking creatively about the future.* It can be hard for a company whose core businesses are highly successful and profitable to recognize the need for new business development; the temptation is to concentrate on what is already successful, and to devote the organization's resources to maintaining that success. However, focusing on just one side of the equation is too great a risk for any business to take.

## Combining Strategic Planning and Strategy Making: Why You Need Both

At its worst, allowing strategy to emerge—waiting for the market to dictate strategy—can be dangerously similar to just muddling through: Hey, we haven't got a plan, but we'll see what's happening and then react to it. We'll keep in touch with what's going on out there, and hope we can catch the wave.

14

Companies without a strong sense of direction, who simply try to respond to what is happening in their markets, can wind up with no core identity. Fluidity should not mean having no shape at all, or changing shape whenever the outside environment changes. That in itself is demoralizing for employees.

At the other extreme, formal, deliberate strategic planning can mean a long cumbersome process that, given today's business climate, simply takes too long for relevant information to filter through. In an increasingly volatile, competitive environment, day-to-day information about what customers want, what competitors can do, and how a company's products and services stack up is absolutely critical. But in many organizations, this information may never get to the designated strategists at the top. As the economist Kenneth Boulding said (and as many people who work in corporations would agree), "The very purpose of a hierarchy is to prevent information from reaching higher layers. It operates as an information filter, and there are little wastebaskets all along the way."[8]

Even when the information arrives in the CEO's office, several factors may be at work to prevent its being acted on in a speedy fashion. It is hard, after all, to abandon a whole way of thinking, or an approach that may have worked well for the business for years, on the basis of some new information. The very fact of having arrived at the top tends to make senior managers feel that they know best, but what worked brilliantly in the past may not work in the future. It is the people on the front lines—the ones least insulated from ordinary customers—who are most likely to catch the first whiff of changing needs. As David Murphy, vice president of human resources at Ford Motor Company, put it, "We can't afford to wait for decisions to come down from the top. If we did, the consumer would be [angry] about having to wait so long—and would be gone before those decisions even got made."[9]

What if the process of arriving at strategy could include both the coherent sense of direction that deliberate strategy provides and the flexibility and ability to adapt that are the virtues of allowing strategies to emerge? What if there were a way of capturing the advantages of rational planning processes while still allowing for maximum responsiveness to customers? Can there be institutional processes that allow strategy to emerge informally?

It is not that businesses have to stop formulating plans; they just have to learn to regard these plans differently. It is no longer a question of issuing marching orders to the troops, but of coming up with working papers: something intended to clarify issues and goals, not to be slavishly obeyed. (There are times when the most useful thing about a plan is that it serves to remind people of what they are deviating from!)

The greatest military leaders, despite their reputation as command-and-control figures, have always known this. A recent article in the *Harvard Business Review* pointed out that Admiral Lord Nelson, the hero of the Battle of Trafalgar, actually gave the captains of his fleet more freedom to make their own decisions than they had ever had before. Rather than trying to control their every movement through flag signals back and forth, as Royal Navy commanders usually did, he simply required them to adhere to one basic strategic principle: Always get beside an enemy ship. As long as they obeyed that one central command, they could determine their course of action for themselves, adapting to the particular situation they found themselves in. It worked brilliantly.[10]

For an organization to successfully transform itself—and in today's climate, organizations need to perpetually transform themselves in order to survive—requires a combination of intentional change (the goals defined in the strategic plan, the formal strategies laid out in the binder or the Power Point slides) and responsiveness to what emerges in the process. It may also require recognizing that strategies *are* in fact emerging, that the strategy laid out in the binder is actually not the only one being pursued. Sometimes, a stated strategy may be belied by the way resources are allocated. Intel, for example, went on thinking of itself as a memory company long after much of its manufacturing capacity had been reallocated to microprocessors; a strategy had emerged without being acknowledged.

*Strategy versus tactics.* Accepting the idea that strategy is not always intentional but may emerge, or evolve, over time means recognizing that strategy is not just about planning. It is also about doing—and sometimes the doing actually comes before the planning. That flies in the face of an idea we all learned in school: First plan, then act. While such a neat linear sequence may sound like the rational way to go, in the real world we often act and then use the results of our actions to decide on the next step.

To embrace the idea of emergent strategies calls for a different understanding of the relationship between strategy and tactics. The line between them, which was once considered sharply defined, has increasingly become blurred. When we talk of "evolving strategy" (a term that first appeared in my book *The New Strategists* in 1995), we are accepting that, in the process of implementation, strategies will be continually reshaped, as people at all levels of the organization respond to customers, sign up new clients, work with suppliers, design new products, and refine existing ones. This is more than a matter of tactics, that is, choosing the means to arrive at the end defined by senior management.

In other words, because formulation and implementation cannot be clearly distinguished, and because the rapid pace of change requires frequent adaptation of existing strategies, today's tactics can become the basis of tomorrow's strategy.

Robert Silver, executive vice president of UBS Wealth Management USA, recalls how Corporate Employee Financial Services, an equity administration service for Fortune 500 companies that currently has more than 800,000 participants and nearly 100 corporate clients, got started:

> One of our advisers in Hartford, Connecticut who had a strong advisory relationship with a client started doing it on a small scale locally, since it was something the client needed. We realized it had great potential, and could lead to high asset retention and capture as well as being the best source of lead generation and client contact. So we wound up making a huge investment to professionalize it and make a line of business out of it.[11]

What had begun as a tactic to satisfy the needs of a specific customer emerged into a strategy.

## Strategy Making as a Dynamic Learning Process

Figure 1.1 shows the process of arriving at strategy as a combination of all four of the elements previously discussed. In this model, all the elements and activities feed into each other in a dynamic learning process that has no distinct beginning, middle, or end. It can start at any of the four points depicted in the figure. The sequence of events is less important than being sure to recognize and manage all four aspects of strategy making.

Whether they consciously decide to incorporate all four elements or not, most successful companies leverage this four-part

**Deliberate Strategies** are developed and revised . . .

. . . **Strategic Foresight** based on discovering unanticipated markets and unarticulated customer needs.

. . . and tested for their **Strategic Fit** with customers and markets.

New Strategies also **Evolve** based on the learnings of front-line strategists, leading to . . .

*Figure 1.1*   Strategy as an Ongoing Process

process. A good example is the story of Honda's entry into the U.S. motorcycle market. Originally, Honda's strategy—its deliberate strategy—was to compete directly against Harley-Davidson. In 1959, Honda sent some of their managers to Los Angeles to launch their large motorbikes into the U.S. market. Because they were short of foreign currency and had been told there was no public transport in the city, these managers used Honda's small Super Cub motor scooters to get around.

The company had assumed these small bikes would not be worth marketing in the United States, because of their modest size and lack of luxury, but the big motorcycles they were trying to promote proved to have serious reliability problems. Meanwhile, the Super Cubs kept attracting admiring attention—every time one of the Honda managers parked his bike somewhere, people came up to him and asked where he had bought it. Next, a Sears buyer phoned to inquire about selling the bikes through their organization. At first, Honda resisted, but when it became clear that the problems with the larger bikes meant they could never hope to crack the hard-core motorcycle market, the company finally adopted the promotion of Super Cubs as its deliberate strategy. Before they did so, motorcycles had been seen as strictly the province of the black-leather-jacket crowd. Pretty soon, middle-class Americans were buying Super Cubs from sporting goods stores, and Honda became a highly visible presence in the American market.

In another piece of serendipity, the monumentally successful ad for Super Cub—"You meet the nicest people on a Honda"—was conceived by an undergraduate advertising major at UCLA as a class project. His instructor took it to his neighbor, a Honda executive, who brought it into the company. Honda was initially reluctant to use it; they didn't want to offend the leather-jacketed motorcycle crowd. Only the dogged persistence of the sales director convinced them to run the student's ad, after which sales went through the roof. A classic piece of strategic foresight, the ad played a big role in tapping into the demand for small motorbikes, which had gone unidentified before.

## Overhauling the Planning Process

When 13 supervisors at International Harvester took on massive debt to buy a failing division of the company that rebuilt heavy engines and their components, they realized that the survival of their new business, the Springfield Remanufacturing Corporation (SRC), would depend on all their employees understanding its finances. Each of the company's 199 employees was given shares of stock, at $.10 apiece; in addition they were all invited into the weekly huddles in which the financial data was looked at and sales and profit targets were set: Those who could not understand income statements and balance sheets were given training in how to do so.

The looming prospect of imminent disaster (Springfield's debt-to-equity ratio was a staggering 89 to 1) inspired a planning ritual, based around the huddles, that focused SRC on controlled growth, orderly operations, predictability, and wealth creation. CEO Jack Stack involved every SRC employee in the weekly planning and monitoring process, and established a bonus system based on meeting the targets for the plan, which was highly sales driven.

In order to ensure that all employees would have enough information to make effective strategic decisions, Stack also pioneered what came to be known as "open-book management." Everyone at Springfield had complete access to the company's financial data, meaning that strategic decisions could be made at every level. For example, a mechanic who was trying to decide whether to repair an engine's connecting rod or install a new one could compare his wage, $26 per hour, to the cost of a replacement rod, $45, and figure out that only if the job could be completed in under 90 minutes would it make sense to fix the old one.[12] Each employee was encouraged to think about the business in terms of opportunities for revenue generation and the management of expenditure, including their own salaries, benefits, and bonuses.

Within 3 years of its founding, Springfield Remanufacturing was turning a profit; within 10 years its stock—more than 80 percent of which was owned by employees—had gone up by 18,200 percent.[13]

## The Role of Strategic Teams

It is only natural for people to focus on the kind of information that is most relevant to their own jobs. A marketing manager will pay more attention to feedback on markets; an R&D engineer will be particularly tuned in to news of scientific advances or inklings of scientific problems. Both will probably have blind spots, or know or understand too little about certain areas to recognize relevant information about them. Making sure that all key functions are represented on a given team leads to the kind of balance and objectivity that was once supposed to be the exclusive province of senior management.

Using teams to develop strategy is also a good way of ensuring that strategy making becomes a dynamic learning process. The inevitable flow of information and ideas among team members is itself conducive to both learning and fluidity. Furthermore, combining the different expertise of diverse groups of people increases the chance that no important factor will be overlooked, and all likely obstacles will be foreseen. At General Electric (GE), for example, cross-functional teams include representatives from research, marketing, engineering, and manufacturing and service, as well as vendors and customers.

Similarly, at Northern Telecom, even teams brought together to address a specific business's or function's problems will include people from other areas. A Northern Telecom vice president explains, "We wanted to bring the widest diversity of ideas to each team so we could stimulate breakthrough thinking. If we are working on a manufacturing problem and we just use manufacturing people, the solution won't be nearly as good as it could be."

The very nature of teamwork encourages the evolution of strategy. As people bounce ideas off each other, they tend to refine and develop them as they go along. In the course of their work, they may become aware of trends or customer needs that are just beginning to surface, or have not yet been identified. In fact, strategic foresight can sometimes be a matter of putting together two, three, or four different perceptions or hunches, realizing that what A has noticed about one group of customers may link up with what B has noticed about another. If creativity is about making connections between seemingly unlike things, as is often argued, the more heads you can put together, the more connections are likely to get made.

## Self-Generated Teams

Perhaps the most productive teams of all are those that have not been designated by upper management, but that come together on their own initiative because people are interested in finding new ways of doing things, or have an idea they want to develop. Organizations are beginning to encourage this kind of "self-organization" at all levels, gambling on productive outcomes from such grass-roots teams. (That means, among other things, learning to accept the inevitability of failure—because not all ideas will come to fruition or prove profitable—rather than punishing people for it.)

At W.L. Gore & Associates, project teams evolve from employee initiatives. Employees who think they have a good idea are expected to act like independent entrepreneurs and try to rally colleagues behind it. If enough people share the employee's enthusiasm, a project team is born. Usually the person who first conceived of the idea becomes the project leader, although other team members can decide to appoint someone else. Any worker, at any level of the organization, can become a team manager.[14]

At Sumitomo 3M, engineer Kazunori Kondoh was intrigued rather than dismayed when it turned out that a microporous film

23

intended for use in safety garments darkened after repeated contact with human skin. While others in the company considered it a flaw that the product was highly absorbent of skin oils, Kondoh saw an opportunity to create a new kind of facial skin treatment. Because his 3M colleagues did not immediately share his enthusiasm, he became a one-man cheering squad for the idea, developing his own production system, meeting with 3M marketing people and customers. Finally, he was able to put a team together, and his product—a new line of skin care applications, bought by a major cosmetics company—was an immediate market success.[15]

## The Role of Senior Managers

We've just seen some examples of strategy making at its most dynamic, as a process that goes on at all levels of an organization. When strategies emerge from that kind of dynamic learning process, the role of senior management changes. Instead of setting the company's direction in a specific, step-by-step way, and trying to control it from on high, senior managers are more likely to concentrate on formulating a general strategy that is based on input from people at all levels of the organization as well as their own insights.

The task of formulating specific plans for the business units can be handed over to lower-level employees, although senior managers will still be responsible for monitoring progress and ensuring that the company is really moving in the direction of greater responsiveness. Their role is to offer guidance and keep things on track, not to lay down the law. At the same time, they should be using the insights and knowledge of those on the front lines to hone their own strategic foresight.

Rather than being all-powerful parent figures responsible for setting the strategic direction of their companies single-handedly—as the business press likes to depict them—senior managers need to become elder-brother/sister figures instead. It may not be coincidental that the call for more participative strategy making comes at a time when not only is it necessary to respond more quickly to market changes, but people are increasingly reluctant to obey orders unquestioningly.

## In Conclusion

We have seen that the dynamic learning process known as strategy making can and should involve both deliberate planning and allowing strategies to emerge; it can and should encompass both strategic fit and strategic foresight. The challenge is to get past either-or thinking and find ways to incorporate all the benefits of different approaches to strategy within the same process. In the chapter that follows, we look at some of the dilemmas—the seemingly either/or choices—that organizations face when trying to design an inclusive strategy-making process.

## Key Points

- To succeed, businesses have to make use of both strategic fit and foresight. That is, they have to ensure that they can serve customers' current needs as efficiently and effectively as possible while also thinking creatively about the future.
- Businesses require both the coherent sense of direction that deliberate strategy provides and the flexibility and

ability to adapt that they gain from allowing strategies to emerge. The challenge is to maintain focus while achieving maximum responsiveness to customers. Though it may seem paradoxical, organizational systems and processes can be designed to encourage innovation and the emergence of strategy.

- With emergent strategy, planning and doing can no longer be neatly separated; as people at all levels of the organization go about their business of implementing strategies, the strategies themselves take on different shapes. Thus, the line between strategies and tactics increasingly becomes blurred.
- Cross-functional teams are an invaluable part of the new kind of strategy making. Not only are the solutions arrived at more inclusive and balanced, but the sharing of information and ideas makes for a dynamic learning process.

# 2 | Challenges in Strategy Making

The process of arriving at success often involves reconciling seemingly opposite demands. Not too long ago, for example, it was thought that companies could compete either by achieving economies of scale, that is, making lots of widgets that were all the same, at the lowest possible cost; or through differentiation, that is, making specialized widgets for specific markets that were willing to pay more for them. For many organizations, however, it is now not only possible but necessary to compete by doing both simultaneously: flexible manufacturing on a large scale. (This is the "mass customization" strategy for which Dell is famous: building computers customized to each customer's specifications within a few days of the time the order is placed.) Rather than choosing between one good idea and another, they have arrived at a synthesis that incorporates the best features of both.

Keep the idea of synthesis in mind as you consider the following dilemmas:

- Inviting more people to participate in strategic decision making will mean the process will take longer. Isn't the

goal to make decisions faster in order to be more responsive to the market?

- If everyone in the organization is involved in strategy
  making, won't that mean that nobody is really in charge?
  Who makes the final decisions, the judgment calls? Are we
  supposed to get rid of hierarchy altogether?
- How can the organization maintain a clear strategic focus
  if people are constantly running after new opportunities
  and trying to tap into unidentified markets?

The conflicts these questions bring to light are real ones. But
the either/or mentality is damaging to creativity and progress
alike. Remember the notion of functional chaos discussed in
Chapter 1: Part of being in a state of continuous disequilibrium
is juggling seemingly opposite demands and imperatives, adapting to seemingly irreconcilable needs.

Are there more inclusive ways in which these conflicts can be
resolved? Let us look at them one at a time.

*Dilemma 1: Involving more people in strategic decision-making
takes longer. Isn't the goal to make decisions faster in order to be
more responsive to the market?*

In many organizations, wider participation in strategy making translates into more meetings, more politics, more memos,
more signoffs. (One commentator described the situation like
this: "People were busy all day about being busy. Morning and
afternoon they held meetings and wrung from themselves the
decision to hold other meetings on the same subjects but on different days.") So senior managers fear that broader involvement

will lead only to endless thrashing around and an inability to make responsive decisions.

What if you rephrase the question? Instead of assuming that you can have either broader participation or speed of response, try asking, "How can we get more people involved in strategy making in *order* to make decisions faster in response to the marketplace?"

## Broader Accountability for Strategy Making

As we saw earlier, one way to involve more people in creating strategy, may be, paradoxically, to get corporate executives out of the process of developing specific strategies for business units. Some organizations have adopted a system whereby senior management scopes out an issue and then hands it off to a cross-functional team. Team members assess the overall, general goal and then decide on a more specific team goal. They must then go out and get the support of their functional departments, which are expected to adjust their own goals to the team's; if necessary, these departments also alert the team and/or senior management to potential difficulties or conflicts in priorities. Management then adjusts the company's goals or reexamines issues in line with what the team or the functional department has determined.

During the mid-1990s, Dow Chemical embarked on a process of delayering that reduced the hierarchy from many layers of management to just six, ranging from chief executive officer (CEO) William Stavropoulos to the most junior employee. The primary objective of this delayering, according to Stavropoulos, had everything to do with creating a more responsive organization. As fewer organizational layers called for increased accountability and responsibility, Dow instituted formal programs of empowerment to ensure that employees played a more active role in the decision-making process. Business development managers became part of the business management team as well as champions of new products and processes. Says Stavropoulos, "This changed the stature of the business development people in the company, which allowed them the freedom and the authority to expedite new projects."[1]

At Corning, where layers of bureaucracy that separated technologists from those who control spending have also been eliminated, an even more radical approach has been tried. Doug Hall, for example, a research scientist, became both the strategist/planner and the tactician/doer when he successfully urged development of a product that was the outgrowth of an idea originating in his lab. To speed up the time for getting the product to market, Hall agreed to leave aside his own research temporarily for the managerial job of research supervisor. Hall also paid sales calls: He visited customers and began finding out just what they would want from such a product. When the project was ready to go into pilot production, he and his team rented temporary space outside the Corning facility and worked in isolation, becoming their own company within a company. Once the product was in commercial production, the team dispersed and Hall moved back to the lab. Such total project ownership—and such moves between the business and research sides—are not uncommon at Corning, generally acknowledged as one of the most innovative companies around.[2]

At Merck Pharmaceuticals, worldwide, cross-functional business strategy teams have been created in order, as CEO Ray Gilmartin says, "to keep the decision making at the lowest possible level in the organization, so we can move quickly and not create bottlenecks by pushing everything up to the top." The teams are empowered to make decisions on their own markets and products, with forums in place for resolving issues and problems as quickly as possible.[3]

Many companies besides Merck are making the transition to customer-focused, cross-functional teams in order to get better decisions made faster. For example, an international cross-functional team is credited with making dramatic changes in one major corporation's packaging materials in less than six months. Several years ago, logistics experts who had been in touch with the organization's business center in Germany identified what could become a significant problem. European countries were considering legislation that would require providers of goods to arrange for the disposal of their products' packaging. If this legislation were enacted, consumers would no longer be able to dispose of packaging materials with their regular trash.

Without waiting for a mandate from above, the logistics people pulled together an international team of experts in environmental affairs, purchasing, quality assurance, technical documentation, and even public relations. The packaging team members, who began by evaluating the current packaging materials, were surprised to find that the business was shipping a million cardboard cartons each month. The real problem, however, lay not with the cardboard, which was recyclable, but with other materials, namely Styrofoam and plastic bubble wrap. Within six months, the team had implemented a program to change the packaging. Thanks to their efforts, customers were enabled to recycle more than 6 million cardboard boxes and 48 million semiconductor packaging tubes every year, and the use of plastic bubble packaging was totally eliminated in Europe.

Cross-functional teams, which allow for all aspects of the development process to be addressed simultaneously, have also been invaluable in fostering the development of business strategies by keeping more people in touch with both new technologies and market needs. In some organizations, they have meant reductions in product development time of up to 75 percent. Pfizer, for example, the international pharmaceuticals company, decreased the time it took to get a product to market from two years to six months by developing a team-based culture that would act on early-stage research, rather than waiting until all the approvals were in.

Says Dr. Henry McKinnell, president of Pfizer Pharmaceuticals and CEO of Pfizer, Inc.:

> If you look forward, what you see is expiration of the patents on the products you are currently marketing, and therefore declining sales. So what you know for sure is that the products you are currently selling, like Viagra for example, will be a fraction of their current level over the next two to ten years. In fact, if you look out beyond ten years, you don't have a business . . . What that does strategically, if you have reasonable growth goals, is that it drives you to reinvent yourself two or three times every eight to ten years.[4]

Another way to speed up the process of development while still increasing participation levels is to ensure that people in different parts of the company are able and encouraged to talk to each other, as well as to customers and suppliers. Dr. Lewis S. Edelheit, senior vice president (SVP) of GE, says, "Boundary-busting is how I spend the bulk of my time and energy. . . . I'm confident that our people now understand that we must not construct boundaries within our company."[5]

Kodak's Office of Innovation, which at the time of its founding was the only such corporate center of its kind, not only helps employees get seed grants for pursuing their own projects, it also puts them in touch with others in the company who are interested in the product, technology, or marketing innovation they are experimenting with. Kodak's highly profitable 3-D imaging system, for example, was born when a Kodak employee who had been trying to find a way for his children to make their own 3-D cards was put in touch with other Kodak employees with similar interests. It took several false starts and a number of discouragements, but the innovation center kept the project alive by continuing to put all the company's employees who were interested in 3-D imaging in touch with each other.[6]

## Two-Way Communication

To ensure that the day-to-day decisions made by cross-functional teams and the deliberate strategies that are typically formulated by the organization's strategic leaders are in synch with each other, a formal but flexible system of two-way communication is needed. The two-way aspect is important—it is not enough for the teams to be told what the business's deliberate or overall strategies are, and to be asked to ensure that their decisions are in keeping with them. Teams and individuals also need direct access to senior people, to be able to get important and relevant information to them without going through a hierarchical maze.

In addition, strategic leaders must be prepared to modify strategies in keeping with the news from the front lines. Whether that news relates to a particular product the team is working on or a bulletin on what the competition is up to, a readiness to adapt strategies to reality has to be built into the corporate culture.

## Global Responsiveness

Among the Kodak people who came together to explore the possibilities in 3-D imaging, there happened to be employees from several different countries and different continents. In other cases, such global linkups have become a matter of deliberate policy, to ensure that the organization stays in touch with markets and customers around the world.

At Becton Dickinson, a New Jersey manufacturer of high-tech medical equipment, eight strategic planning teams were made responsible in the 1990s for continually setting and implementing strategies for their divisions. Chuck Baer, then–president of the Consumer Products Division, was a member of his unit's planning team; so were representatives from various functions and locations throughout the world. The team met twice a year in person and much more frequently via conference calls.

Becton Dickinson's managers learned from experience that, in order to be a truly worldwide competitor, they had to enlist global participation in strategy making. "The early strategies," Baer says, "were primarily U.S. based, and for the most part, very little input from outside the U.S. was considered. . . . developments from outside the U.S. didn't find their way into our strategies. We were also not able to develop strategies that might meet needs that were different from the needs of people in the U.S."

Once there was international involvement in the strategy-making process at Becton Dickinson, Baer says, "By sensing what was going on around the world, we could be sure not to get blindsided by anybody who might be creating something in one part of the world but not another. And if we found some development from R&D and some manufacturing opportunities, then we could immediately pull a team together and decide what we wanted to do. This enabled us not only to take advantage of something we developed, but to react quickly to any threat we might see."

At Bell Labs, using "virtual teams" of researchers from all over the world enables products to come to market more quickly by taking advantage of the different kinds of technical expertise available in different locations. But it also makes it possible for products to emerge in ways that will make them attractive in more than a single region. The MiLife 3G, for example, a third-generation cellular mobile Internet platform, was developed by a virtual team located in disparate locations around the world. The team members advised each other not only on the technical aspects of the product but on which features should be included to satisfy consumers in different countries. As Stacey Gelman, Bell Labs' vice president of Mobile Internet, puts it, "The point of MiLife is the end-user experience." The platform allows users to check stock quotes, listen to their e-mail, consult horoscopes, even bet on the day's races, but what is important to end-users differs from country to country. As Gelman says, "The French want applications that promote direct international contact, whereas games and music and time-passers are intensely valuable in the Japanese mobile culture. By contrast, the evolving mobile Internet market in the U.S. isn't into leisurely surfing, but is into highly focused access for specific bits of information, like a high-way report or a stock quote."[7]

*Dilemma 2: If everyone in the organization is involved in strategy making, won't this mean that nobody is really in charge? Who makes the final decisions, the judgment calls? Are we supposed to get rid of hierarchy altogether?*

Wider involvement can succeed only if the traditional hierarchy of strategy making is deemphasized, and employees are empowered to initiate action. However, organizations will always need a way to ensure that strategic decisions are rational, likely to succeed, and consistent with their overall direction. That means there have to be mechanisms in place for containing risk and for coordinating and aligning efforts across the organization.

There is no way to eliminate hierarchy altogether. Somebody will have to make the final judgment call, but although that may sound disempowering, in practice it can actually free employees to air—and act on—their ideas more confidently, protected by the knowledge that, whatever the outcome, it will not spell disaster for the business. (The first time the term "management by objectives" appeared in print, the full phrase used was "management by objectives for self-control.") When people know not only what they are responsible for but also the limits of that responsibility, they feel more comfortable taking risks and trying new ideas; they need to feel sure that, however empowered they are, they do not have the power to destroy the organization. It is the all-important difference between freedom and anarchy.

The simple knowledge that checks and balances exist also confers a kind of freedom. It is reassuring to know that someone else is going to take a look, step back, make a judgment, and suggest modifications and corrections. The challenge is to design systems and structures that allow room for creativity and experimentation while at the same time ensuring that good decisions get made.

If hierarchy frees people to act on their intuitions and ideas, it also serves another very useful purpose: It allows a large organization to be divided into smaller component parts. Without a formal structure or hierarchy, discrete manageable subunits would be impossible. Such smaller units give people a greater sense of belonging and responsibility for results. Hierarchy shows how the subunits are related to each other and to the workings of the overall enterprise. The challenge for subunits is to retain clarity about their roles and responsibilities while also enjoying the flexibility to cross organizational boundaries as necessary to address customer needs and new opportunities.

In many organizations today, the villain is not actually hierarchy but bureaucracy, defined by a dictionary as "a system of administration marked by officialism, red tape and proliferation." As Peter Neff, CEO of the French pharmaceutical giant Rhone–Poulenc's U.S. subsidiary, has remarked, "Bureaucracy is its own worst enemy. It inhibits people from doing their jobs and stifles ideas that can give customers what they need."[8] But having a hierarchy does not automatically mean getting bogged down in bureaucracy, especially when the hierarchy is slimmed down and made flatter, as in so many of today's horizontal organizations. The leaner the hierarchy, the less danger there is that the flab of bureaucracy will build up around it.

The question is not, How can we get rid of hierarchy? We don't want to do that! The question is, How can we use hierarchical structures to foster more participation in strategy making—and more creativity and risk taking in the formulation of strategy?

Not only each industry but each company is different, and no single formula works equally well across the board. Different types of decision-making processes and different degrees of autonomy will be needed from one organization to another, but some sort of balance will always be required. Cumbersome approval processes have to be eliminated, for example, if people at

> The degree of hierarchy required for empowerment—and for clarity and coordination—will vary from company to company, depending on several factors:
>
> - The nature and variety of businesses in the portfolio.
> - The number and types of markets that they serve.
> - The need for an overarching corporate identity in the minds of customers and shareholders.
> - The corporation's existing capital condition.
> - The culture of the company and of the units within it.

all levels of the organization are to see themselves as strategists and entrepreneurs; they not only make timely implementation impossible, which damages the company's competitiveness, but also erode motivation. Yet improbable ideas need to be filtered out, and potential risk needs to be contained.

At Pfizer, there is a highly effective system in place for what Pfizer people term "managing innovation." This is how Dr. John Niblack, former SVP of Research and Development (now Vice Chairman of Pfizer, and President of Pfizer Global Research and Development), describes the process: "In our research division, just as in the rest of the corporation, we emphasize speed. In order to facilitate our processes, we have reduced the number of management levels that separate the sales force and research chemists from the chairman. As senior management people retire or resign, we no longer replace them. We want to eliminate bureaucratic impediments to fast decision-making and immediate action. We want to move power down through the organization."

At the same time, Pfizer's approval process is designed to ensure that only viable projects get supported. As Niblack says,

"Pfizer makes its living selling pharmaceuticals. We cannot afford to chase any leads—no matter how intriguing—that are unlikely to pay off. If a project starts to founder, we end it. Fast."[9]

Dr. Joseph Miller, the former chief technology officer and SVP for Research and Development at DuPont, describes his approach as follows:

> Our scientists . . . value their independence and the license to resist managers' efforts to redirect or otherwise control their work. [Yet] DuPont is determined to have research conform to our strengths and market needs, recognizing that some independence of choice is essential to sustain motivation . . . I endeavor to lay out the strategic areas where research can most benefit the company: areas where the costs are reasonable and the risks acceptable. From that point we define targets. Our researchers arc free to pursue their own goals as they will, with the understanding that we monitor their progress and, at various stages, will weigh the value of continuing their efforts.[10]

3M has a "15 percent rule." That means all their technical people are allowed to spend 15 percent of their time working on projects of their own choosing. They do not have to get approval from anyone, or even tell their managers what they have chosen to work on, but the decision on which projects will proceed to the development phase is up to management.[11]

At IBM's Research Division, as long as their project goals are met, researchers in the division are free to spend their time on projects of their choice. At one point, several separate researchers became interested in using information technology to improve education in grades K–12. Unbeknownst to each other, they began working on the initial, unfunded stages of their different projects. Some, acting on their own initiative, went out and met with people in the schools to get a clearer picture of their needs.

Upon reviewing the yearly project descriptions that these researchers submitted, senior management discovered that there were several related projects underway in the area of education. That prompted them to develop an R&D strategy for the K–12 education market, a strategy that focused and integrated the work already being done in the division. The hierarchical system became the means for turning emergent strategy into deliberate strategy.

*Dilemma 3: How can we maintain a clear strategic focus if everyone is constantly running after new opportunities presented by our customers and markets?*

A surefire recipe for organizational chaos—and not the kind that results in success—is to have everyone working diligently, but at cross purposes. It's the corporate equivalent of the dream about running desperately in place, and it likewise means the company will go nowhere.

How can you maintain the focus on key strategies and still remain open to new opportunities? How can people be empowered to make decisions without running the risk that those decisions will not be aligned with where the company wants to go strategically? One executive calls this dilemma "the necessary tension between autonomy and integration." Again, let us try rephrasing the question to include both components: How can an organization maintain strategic focus *by* remaining open to new opportunities?

When strategy is defined not as something fixed in stone, but as a broad aim or principle, achieving the balance becomes easier. Ongoing dialogue is the key. People need to be asked (and to ask themselves), How does this project, the pursuit of this new opportunity, fit in with the overall strategic focus? At the same time, top management needs to be asked (and to ask itself), Are the strategies we have already selected the only ones that will support our strategic focus?

When there are new developments in the environment, or if all competitors are simultaneously trying to replicate and differentiate, strategies may change even if strategic focus does not. If the overall strategy is to be responsive to customers, for example, a whole new initiative that responds to an unexpected customer need may be perfectly aligned with that strategy, even if it was not part of the original plan. Constant attention needs to be paid to changes—in technology, in customer behavior, in the company's markets, in the actions of competitors—that indicate a need for a shift in strategy. New opportunities that present themselves should also be looked at from a broad perspective; they may indicate environmental shifts that could have far-reaching implications for strategy. Keep in mind, too, that, as noted earlier, planning and doing are not two separate activities. Strategic focus can itself evolve through actions taken to respond to new opportunities.

## Strategy as Dialogue

If strategic focus is constantly evolving, ongoing dialogue is the means of defining it for people in the organization as a dynamic, not a static, thing. As Eccles and Nohria point out, strategy is essentially language, and the broad words typically used to define a business's strategic direction are interpreted differently by different people.[12] Take, for example, the strategy of becoming a global company. The top management teams may say that the company needs to become more global in scope in order to compete in a changing industry. But globalization can take many different forms, and as the various business units find and evaluate opportunities in new geographical arenas, the strategy will be refined. Ask yourself: Do you expand in areas with the biggest market potential? Do you follow existing major customers to serve them in all their locations? Do you create relatively independent units run and staffed by foreign nationals? Do you try to export your "home country" systems and culture? Do you expand alone or through joint ventures with companies that may have more experience in these markets? Finally, do all business units try to go global in the same way?

While answers to these questions may be thought out in advance by senior executives, it is more likely that they will emerge from action. As you try to refine various approaches, the strategy of globalization will be shaped to fit the strengths and culture of the specific company. For example, some years ago ConAgra shifted its globalization strategy, closing the independent unit it had created to lead its push abroad and delegating the responsibility to expand overseas to its individual companies, which best know their own markets.[13]

It is only through ongoing dialogue that people at all levels really come to understand the specific form of globalization that the business is pursuing. This dialogue includes talk about which opportunities were pursued and which were not, the rationale behind those choices, and the ongoing status of various new ventures in different arenas. Such dialogue actually serves to focus the organization's strategy more clearly, rather than allowing the multitude of possible choices to lead to strategic diffusion and *non*functional chaos.

## Strategic Focus as a Moving Target

Since, as we have seen, new possibilities can mean a shift in the strategic direction, the issue becomes not just how to maintain focus but how to recognize when it's time to change it. Outdated or misguided focus—that is, sticking doggedly to what worked in the past, never mind that everything else has changed—can be worse than none at all. Denying or ignoring the need for a new approach is a natural human reaction. It is not easy to "unlearn" old ideas and old ways of going about things. In fact, it is much more difficult than learning from scratch, which is why, despite their lack of in-house experience, new companies often have a huge advantage over established ones: They do not have anything to unlearn before they start learning.

IBM and Digital Equipment discovered this the hard way when they were left behind because of their tunnel-vision strategic focus on mainframe computers. More recently, the bankruptcy of venerable Polaroid was a case of a company that could not reinvent itself. Polaroid was actually one of the first companies to develop digital-imaging technology, but it decided not to try to market it. As one commentator put it, "Polaroid had long relied on a razors-and-blades approach to business: It sold cameras for relatively little and made money on the film. The company couldn't fit digital technologies into that box, so it gave up on digital initiatives and lost its advantage in those technologies to competitors such as Kodak and Fuji."[14]

Bill Gates, on the other hand, was determined from the start that Microsoft would not make the same mistake: "We will not fall short," he said, "for not having an expansive view of how technology can be used."[15]

Such an expansive view can be achieved only by actively searching out new opportunities—opportunities that are not necessarily consistent with existing strategies. For example, CIBT, Inc., a provider of visa, passport, and other international travel services in McLean, Virginia, received a call from a potential customer who was looking for a way to streamline the process for obtaining visas for employees being sent overseas. From the description of the problem, CIBT realized that what was required was a software program that would make the process faster and simpler.

Although the company was not in the software business at the time, it decided to go ahead and launch an initiative to develop such a program. A few years later, the project had evolved into a proprietary system that enabled the company to capture more revenues from a number of major customers.[16]

It stands to reason that when more people are on the lookout for such possibilities, more opportunities will be unearthed or generated. Sometimes, that can mean sifting through thousands of not-so-great ideas to find the ones that can help give the company a competitive advantage. Some companies also offer financial incentives to employees who identify new strategic opportunities.

## Holding onto Valuable, Knowledgeable Employees

Another advantage of encouraging people at all levels of the organization to seek out new opportunities is its effect on a company's ability to hold on to its brightest, most creative employees. Gaining the commitment of the new breed of employees, who want more control over their work lives and more say in how their companies operate, has to involve higher levels of empowerment. And retaining such highly skilled people is becoming increasingly important in a business environment in which knowledge, creativity, skills—intellectual capital—are often a company's chief asset. (According to Baruch Lev, known as the "father of intangible valuation," the annual U.S. investment in intangible assets—R&D, business processes and software, brand enhancement, employee training, and so on—was roughly

$1.0 trillion in the late 1990s, almost equal to the $1.2 trillion total investment of the manufacturing sector in physical assets, while intangible capital currently constitutes between one-half and two-thirds of corporate market value, of both old and New Economy enterprises.)[17]

Genuine empowerment, that is, giving people at all levels real influence on strategy making, has been demonstrated to increase retention rates. When a manager of two 7-Eleven stores in Texas restructured the store clerk's job to include making decisions on which products to keep or discontinue, and how many to order, the results were dramatic: The average tenure of employees increased to four years, compared to an average of 30–60 days for the industry as a whole. When Bank of America allowed the customer service reps in two of their contact centers to redesign their own jobs, there was a 14 percent drop in agent turnover in one of the centers in the first year alone. Furthermore, customer service ratings for the two centers improved by 4.2 percent.[18]

At Leeds Marriott, in Great Britain, all customer service associates attend a program called Spirit to Serve, in which they learn what it is like to be a customer and how their link to customers is vital to the success of the business. Says Human Resources Manager Catherine Waddle, "We also give them the responsibility to look after the customer in any way they see fit, which goes beyond empowerment. They could give a customer a free night at the hotel or a free meal if they saw that the complaint or disruption warranted it. Giving people responsibility shows them how important their role really is." The program has helped Leeds Marriott both to recruit staff and to retain their people once they have been hired.[19]

Yet the issue of empowerment, too, raises certain dilemmas for organizations, as we will examine in Chapter Three.

## Key Points

- One way to get better decisions made faster can be to get senior managers out of the process and leave it to cross-functional teams.
- Two-way communication is vital for ensuring that day-to-day decisions are aligned with organizational strategy, and that organizational strategy is adapted to reflect new information coming in via the front lines.
- Global teams can help ensure responsiveness to many different markets.
- Processes need to be in place that allow for independent action and foster innovation while still filtering out unlikely ideas, or those that are not aligned with the organization's overall strategy.
- Ongoing dialogue about strategy, and how day-to-day actions and decisions align with the company's overall direction, is key. As new opportunities emerge, specific strategies may change even if the strategic focus does not. Only through constant dialogue will it become clear which opportunities should be pursued, which ideas should be explored, and which should not.

# 3 | The Dilemma of Empowerment

Most businesses nowadays recognize that they really cannot afford *not* to empower their people. Apart from the fact that no company can hope to respond rapidly to market changes if it waits for the insights and information coming from the front lines to filter all the way up to senior management, there is also the issue of employees' own expectations. The days when you could expect people to follow orders rather than operate as independent thinkers are gone for good.

However, too often organizations seem only to be paying lip service to the idea of empowerment, rather than energetically putting it into practice. Employee involvement programs, self-directed work groups, team-based organizations: All these may be launched without really giving employees more influence over the direction of the company. In some cases, teams are treated as information gatherers, presenting the facts to senior management. In others, they are empowered to make only trivial decisions, like where to hold the company picnic. Or a team might make what is supposed to be a significant decision, only to find that it has been overruled by more senior people.

That type of incomplete or token empowerment can be particularly harmful if it means that people do not get to decide how they do their own work. If they have no confidence that their decisions will be implemented, they will start to feel that their real objective is not to create strategy but to come up with presentations that please senior management. The less they believe that their ideas will be translated into reality, the more they will resent the additional work.

It is also not sufficient simply to hold meetings where strategies are communicated to lower-level managers in order to gain their commitment. No matter how well you communicate, you cannot make people believe that it is their strategy if they hear about it only after it has already been adopted.

Even—or it might be more accurate to say, especially—when downsizing is required, companies are discovering the benefits of wider involvement in strategy making. Such benefits include strategies that better reflect the realities of the market and the company's strengths, greater buy-in from those responsible for implementing the strategies, and a deeper understanding of those strategies at all levels of the organization. While it may not seem as though employees will willingly contribute to strategies that could lead to the loss of their own or their colleagues' jobs, they are in fact far more likely to accept such an outcome when they have been asked to participate in making the decision.

Employees who feel that their organization treats empowerment efforts as just so much window dressing are inclined to locate the problem in senior management's reluctance to relinquish power. Although that may be a factor, the fact is that genuine empowerment of employees is a mammoth and complex challenge, one that many organizations are not sure how to handle.

This chapter addresses questions such as the following: How

do you manage risk in a situation in which everyone is empowered to make decisions? How do you decide who is responsible for what? How can you maintain enough control to retain strategic focus? How do you structure the process of handing over responsibility to others? What kind of guidance do you need to provide?

## Risk Management

Obviously, there have to be mechanisms in place that will stop a proposal for something like curry-flavored whiskey from getting to the stage where people's time and the organization's money are wasted. Again, it is a matter of finding the balance between control and freedom, of encouraging experimentation and innovation while ensuring continued profitability. Risks have to be taken—and there are bound to be failures along the way—but there also has to be a sober calculation of the odds.

To minimize the risk to the company, some organizations encourage experimentation on a small scale, thereby limiting the possible damage when a strategic initiative by an employee fails to produce the desired results. Nigel Morris, CEO of Capital One, whose own big idea for revolutionizing the credit card industry—offering consumers varying rates, payment options, and other services—was rejected by 20 banks before he found a taker, has adopted this approach to nurturing entrepreneurs while protecting the company's core business.

Several years ago, a group of employees approached him with a plan to set up an operation in London. "A lot of people told me the English would not be interested in our products, because they were used to dealing with big name banks that they knew and trusted," Morris told an interviewer. Nevertheless, he allowed the employees to go ahead on a limited scale.

The response rate was, he says, beyond his highest expectations, and Capital One is now building a full-scale British credit-card operation.[1]

When Southwest Airlines clerks suggested doing away with tickets long before other airlines had adopted electronic ticketing, then-CEO Herb Kelleher encouraged them to experiment with the idea on a few selected routes. The result was lower costs and shorter loading times. Southwest later extended the practice to all the airlines' routes.[2]

At UBS, according to chief information officer (CIO) Scott Abbey, "the strategy is to try things that may be successful, but at the right risk level." Abbey cites the case of a desktop software package for financial advisors that was being redesigned several years ago: "A small percentage of our advisors had dial-up capabilities, and we wanted to replicate that capability in the new version. One of our middle managers suggested using the Internet to achieve this functionality. We went ahead with it without much more review because it had low investment with limited functionality, addressing a small population of users. It evolved into a core strategic project that we were able to sell to other professional clients and now has an installed user base of between five and six thousand."

Abbey also stresses the need to find the right balance between empowerment and setting boundaries, which in the case of the technology department are often about "what technology solutions or standards we will use . . . . The overall spending allocation is on a top-down basis. The work to reconcile the available resources versus the demands is done on a bottom-up basis. Senior management provides guidance and asks, 'Does this project match the strategic model? Does it reduce costs?' "[3]

## The Delegation Dilemma

---

Delegation is part of a continuum: At one end is task assignment; at the other, abdication of responsibility. Delegation, which lies between the two, involves agreeing *what* is to be done, while leaving the choice of the specifics—the *how*—to the individual.

---

It is an old truism that many managers find it easier to do everything themselves than to delegate to others. They may not trust other people to do as good a job as they can, or they may simply not know how to delegate in a way that leads to the results they want. So they feel burdened, and those who work for them feel frustrated and underused.

In a climate of company-wide empowerment, delegation skills are more necessary than ever, yet they are rarely analyzed or taught. The guidelines that follow are based on 20 years of research by Dr. Gary Yukl, a leader in the field of effective management practices.

- *State responsibilities clearly and make sure they are understood.* Explain clearly what the goals of the effort are, what results are expected, and, if it is a specific project, what the deadline for completion is. Ask questions to make sure the other person understands. If the individual or team is inexperienced, or the project is especially complex, it is a

*(Continued)*

good idea to review action plans before they are implemented. Clarity about goals must, however, be balanced with the freedom to improvise. Be clear about what the objective is, but avoid telling people how to accomplish it.

■ *Specify the limits of discretion.* A senior executive put it this way: "The leadership role is to stimulate and channel, which I interpret to mean providing the parameters and some of the limits as well as the encouragement." When delegating new responsibilities, clearly specify the person's or team's limits of discretion—what you expect them to decide for themselves and the kinds of decisions you need to approve. Such authority includes the right to make decisions without prior approval and the right to use funds, equipment, materials, facilities, and other people's time.

■ *Get people involved in deciding on the limits of their discretion.* People will feel more committed if they have a say in how much authority they will have. While employees welcome being given decision-making power, they may not feel comfortable without a clear sense of its limits. Do not force them to take on more responsibility than they are comfortable with. If someone is reluctant to assume more authority, delegate responsibility gradually, allowing the person to build confidence in his or her abilities. As Julia Turney, a senior manager at the financial advisory firm of Partridge Muir & Warren, says, "If you give people tools and information to manage their empowerment, it can be good. But if you don't, they can be left bewildered. And you have to remember that with some people, even if you give them the tools they need, they may still not want it."[4]

After the delegation discussion, take time to do the following:

- *Inform others who need to know.* Tell the people who are affected by the shift in authority, including other people who report to you, peers in other units, your boss, and clients and suppliers. Unless you inform them, these people may have doubts about who is making the decisions.
- *Monitor progress.* Do not assume that once decisions are delegated, you should take yourself out of the loop. It is important to check on progress and provide people with feedback—but do not decide unilaterally how you will track performance and progress toward goals. Rather, arrive at the decision through discussion.
- *Provide the information people will need.* In order to make good decisions, people almost always need additional information. If possible, arrange for such information to flow to them directly, instead of going through you first. Encourage and help people to establish their own sources of essential data through networking, news services, and so on.
- *Give support and help, but avoid "reverse delegation."* Be supportive, especially when people are discouraged or frustrated. However, when they report problems with the delegated project, avoid the very human temptation to

*(Continued)*

jump in with your solution. Instead, ask them to give their recommendations and ideas for how the problem could be solved.

Avoid "reverse delegation," in which you wind up re-asserting control over decisions that have been delegated. You can help people evaluate whether or not their solutions are feasible, but your role should remain that of a resource and consultant, not a decision maker.

As more and more companies recognize the value of what employees at all levels can contribute to the strategy-making process, they have adopted a number of innovative approaches that serve both to empower employees and to resolve the dilemmas such empowerment can present.

## Using Multilevel Teams for Planning

Rather than asking business units and teams at lower levels to develop strategies that must then be approved by senior management, some companies are creating multilevel planning teams that include people from various levels as well as various functions. For example, at Komo Machines, a U.S. maker of machinery for metalworking and cabinetry, employees were invited to apply for work on the strategic planning team. About one-third of them took up the invitation, and 13 team members were selected. While the first such team included the president of the company, it mostly consisted of a cross section of people from all levels of the organization.[5]

At the Tucson Old Pueblo Credit Union of Tucson, Arizona, leaders ranging from the CEO to staff-level employees are sent to two-day strategic planning workshops and then given the task of spearheading a "scenario planning" effort undertaken by a diverse group of teams. The first year after participation in the workshop, the focus was on defining the organization's core values and discussing the possible ways the future might develop. In the following year, teams were set to work defining the credit union's vision and the possible strategic options for each probable future.

Team leaders, who themselves come from all levels of the company, meet to discuss the issues and decide which team should address which area. The teams then explore those areas for a full year. Each team summarizes its findings in November, and an informational packet is distributed and studied in plenty of time before the annual planning meeting in December. At the meeting, all the members of the team—a mix of board members, managers, and staff—report on their function. "The whole process makes the credit union feel more flexible. You see scenarios and early warning signs of environmental changes and can then adjust plans more quickly, not only to survive changes but thrive in them," says Board Chairman Joseph Barkenbush.[6]

At another credit union, Seattle Telco, the president and CEO, Tony Backes, decided to increase staff involvement in strategic planning when dramatic changes seemed necessary. Says Backes, "The larger-group concept allows you to reach conclusions that allow more significant change, and we ended up changing our direction dramatically. Staff buy-in occurred naturally, and people felt wedded to the plan and invested in it."

Seattle Telco's strategic planning team includes branch managers, call center managers, information technology managers, and human resources managers as well as senior people. Rather than merely sitting at a conference table, people are asked to walk around the room, writing their answers to several "big, strategic questions" about the competition, technology, and other issues that have been posted on large charts taped to the walls. The planning group breaks into small teams periodically, to work on specific tasks and report back to the group. Following the presentations, the teams are changed, so that different people wind up giving feedback and suggestions on the original team's work. The original teams then reconvene to consider the ideas that have been proposed.

Shortly after the cross-functional teams come up with a strategic plan, the rest of Seattle Telco's managers and supervisors are bought together and asked for their feedback on the plan before it is presented for board approval. They go through their own, modified version of the planning session, again in cross-functional teams, and their suggestions for additions and changes are incorporated into the plan before it is finalized. Backes sees this process as providing two important benefits: increasing buy-in and improving the quality of the plan itself.[7]

Continental Airways has also invested in employee training and has created multilevel, cross-functional teams to tackle all sorts of strategic issues confronting the airline, from on-time performance to design and development questions to integration planning.[8] In an even more radical scenario, Seagate Technology, a maker of computer hard drives, used multilevel, cross-functional teams to redesign its whole business.

After years of growth and technical leadership, in 1998 the company found itself with slowing sales and dwindling operating income. Craig Nichols, one of a number of consultants brought in from Ernst & Young, recommended that it was time to "transform the whole operations side of the business." His suggestion for how to do so was not to appoint project teams and issue reports, but to select people from all levels of the company, add some consultants, enlist the participation of some customers, and then ask them to come up with a completely new concept of how to run and organize the business—in three days!

Nichols's plan was based on a concept known as DesignShop, developed and trademarked by Matt Taylor, an architect, and his educator wife Gail. DesignShop has been used to plan for radical change by such companies as Hewlett-Packard and Johnson & Johnson, who now—like the U.S. Air Force—have their own, permanent DesignShop facilities. Under the DesignShop scheme, participants are brought to a setting with no conference tables, no auditorium-style seating, only furniture that can be shifted about and walls that move easily, to accommodate the ever-shifting compositions of teams. Puzzles and an eclectic library of books are meant to stimulate creativity and encourage people to break free of preconceived notions.

In Seagate's case, the 80 participants, chosen from all areas and levels of the company, were deliberately combined to include both progressive thinkers and those likely to present barriers to change. As the teams were set up, an employee might find himself playing his boss's boss. One team was to be Seagate, a second IBM, a third a hypothetical capital-rich disk-drive manufacturer named Swarm, and the fourth a company that was a customer of Seagate's (this team included real customers). The result of the intensive three-day experience was a new operating model and a road map for how to get to where they wanted to go. COO William Watkins describes the increased efficiency they achieved: "We were doing 6.5 million drives a quarter, with $800 million in inventory. Now we can do almost double that, with only $400 million."[9]

At AES Corporation, a global electric company based in Arlington, Virginia that has been called "a poster company for empowerment," every team is, in effect, multilevel, or perhaps it would be more accurate to say horizontal: There is so little hierarchy—"we abhor layers," says chairman Roger Sant—that the idea of levels hardly applies. The whole business is organized around small teams, each of which has full responsibility for both maintenance and operations in its area. In fact, apart from an accounting function, there is no corporate staff, no marketing division, no environmental compliance division, no finance group, not even a human resources function. The people at the plant even invest the company's money.

In one facility in Connecticut, all the teams were asked whether they would be interested in investing the $12 million in cash reserves held at their plant. The maintenance crew volunteered, was given responsibility for investing the money, and hired a teacher to help them learn the basics, like who to call to buy and sell shares. After three months of study and practice, they were getting higher returns than the professionals investing the money for the company's treasury.[10]

## Soliciting Broad Input before the Plan Is Finalized

Even in an organization where people at lower levels are involved in creating strategy, the reality is that only a small number of them will actually be there hammering it out. What about the rest of the employees—how can you gain their commitment? And how can you ensure that potentially valuable contributions to any given strategy will not be overlooked?

Although you cannot have everyone in the organization sitting at the table when a strategy is formulated, there are still ways of allowing everyone to participate. One such way is to get as much input as possible from as many people as possible before the strategy is finalized. For example, at Brio Technology, a business intelligence software company in California, 400 of the company's 650 employees were invited to a two-day meeting to respond to and give input on the strategies the company's leadership had tentatively identified. Customers and other stakeholders also participated; the group was divided into different teams and asked to brainstorm around specific areas.

The teams then decided what needed to be added or changed in the proposed strategies as they had been presented. On the evening of the first day, the leadership team revised the draft strategic plan based on people's input. The next morning, they presented their revised plan, and handed out copies of it to each meeting participant. Other components of the agenda were "a panel of possibilities," consisting of representatives of companies who had adopted similar strategies and reported on their experiences, and stations around the room where people could go to find out about the new ideas the company was considering and give their input as desired.[11]

Many other organizations are using large-scale conferences, followed by specific feedback mechanisms, to gather input they can use to develop and refine their strategies. At a U.S. division of a large international corporation, a broad-scale change effort based on a new vision and specific standards of excellence, which also involved a number of layoffs, was introduced at a leadership conference attended by more than 90 managers. Small groups at the conference critiqued the draft of the vision and standards, and their input was incorporated into a second draft. Furthermore, each manager returned to his or her unit and solicited suggestions and reactions that were then recorded and sent back to senior management. Here are some examples of the feedback:

- "I believe in and have conveyed to my people the truly revolutionary opportunity this conference represented—that it was an opportunity for us to participate in a constructive, very real way in the development and implementation of a business plan."
- "Why did it take so long for management to catch up with the rumor mill? The changes have been too slow."
- "Having the organization structured to encourage informal and easy communication across lines of business and quicker, less cumbersome decision-making was especially welcomed."
- "The degree of uncertainty throughout the organization is affecting morale and decision-making."
- "Why are we dismantling a delivery system that wasn't broken? Our heretofore excellent results may be impaired by limited locations and the new 15 percent Return on Capital requirement."
- "The emphasis is on 'trimming'; however, no special consideration appears to be given to dedicated and long-term employees."
- "It was difficult to characterize any broad sentiment. Some people are experiencing a considerable amount of tension, a feeling of anger and disappointment within the organization. Others see this as an opportunity; their only concern is that they will not be recognized for their skills and their ability to learn."

The feedback was used to revise the organization's strategies in order to address concerns and find ways to manage the effects of such a major change on morale and employee retention.

## The Importance of Two-Way Communication

The conference just described was invaluable largely because it provided a forum for two-way communication. If the CEO had simply made a speech, followed by presentations by senior managers, most of its benefit would have been lost. Not only would the attendees have been less likely to feel really committed to implementing the new strategies, but senior managers would have missed the opportunity to get the input and recommendations of lower-level employees. As a result, the strategies themselves would have suffered from not accurately reflecting whatever internal and external realities senior managers were unaware of. For that reason, many leading-edge companies present their strategic plans to employees as works in progress and ask for their reactions.

At Procter & Gamble's Indian subsidiary, for instance, there are open sessions with the CEO where employees are free to raise questions on organizational changes, express their concerns about their roles and the business, and have the CEO and directors reply immediately. Since it is an open forum, known as Let's Talk, any and all questions are allowed. One employee might ask about a hard-core business-related issue, while another might make a request for a gym to be added to a new facility or offer a suggestion about the design of the meeting rooms being built. (In fact, the final layout of the new headquarters was largely an outcome of the discussions at "Let's Talk" sessions.)

Questions can also be submitted anonymously, but as employees see that there are no repercussions when they question senior management's decisions, this becomes less and less necessary. "P&G has found that opening lines of communication focuses employees' energy towards positive output and away from corridor talk. The 'Let's Talk' open sessions are increasing employee feedback on business choices and company policies, helping to deliver a more meaningful face to the external world, and even boosting employee morale," says Anthony Rose, senior manager of public affairs.[12]

## Gathering Input

If listening to people is crucial, so is finding the right channels for that listening. Simply "opening the floor" to extended, un-structured question-and-answer sessions in which 30 or more people stand up and speak is rarely an effective or efficient way to proceed. There are more productive methods for gathering in-put from large groups. For example, you might try one of the following approaches:

- After the proposed strategies have been presented, break the large group into smaller table groups. Give them a format for discussing their reactions to the plans: what they liked, what their concerns are. Ask them to take some time (thirty to forty-five minutes, perhaps) to discuss their reactions and to prepare a brief report-out on a flip chart, listing their top three pluses and concerns. Then return to the large group, and have one represen-tative from each table give a brief summary of their conclusions. At the end of the conference, gather up the flip chart pages and use them to refine the strategies.

- Hold a structured question-and-answer session. Before the session, ask people to submit their questions in writing. The people responding will have time to prepare their answers, and redundant discussion can be eliminated. The floor can then be opened for discussion of any further questions or ideas that have been triggered by the initial response.

- Provide structured, brief questionnaires designed to gather reactions and suggestions about the strategies. These can be completed anonymously, if the organization's culture does not encourage honest, critical feedback, but it is preferable to have respondents identify themselves, so that they can be contacted for clarification and notified of how their concerns are being addressed.

- Give conference participants a format and materials for holding a meeting with people in their organizations who have not attended the session. This can include handouts and/or transparencies to help them explain the proposed strategies to others, questions to generate open and constructive discussion, and a suggested format for relaying suggestions and questions back to the designated strategy makers by a specific date.

- Ask conference participants to volunteer for post-conference task forces to solve specific problems or tackle sticky issues.

---

Gathering input from a broad variety of sources is critical. However, it should never be seen as an end in itself, or it will become just a way to manipulate people's commitment by creating the illusion that their views are being taken into account. (Remember the old cartoon about the suggestion box that opens directly into the wastebasket?) The input must actually be used, or the effect on morale can be worse than if it had not been asked for in the first place.

---

Follow-up communications after a conference should include specific, detailed responses to the ideas generated—which are being implemented, which are not, and why. Specific members of the planning committee can take responsibility for following up on particular issues. At the end of the conference, let people know who will be following up, and the date by which they can expect an update on a particular project or issue. Make sure those commitments are met.

## Tolerating Criticism

One of the features of the leadership conference just described was that the follow-up from senior managers and their people included some blunt criticisms of the change effort that was underway. A tolerance for that type of criticism is crucial to the success of participatory strategy making. In many organizations, long-established patterns of relating must change before employees can feel comfortable voicing their criticisms. Such a change will not happen overnight.

People who have seen their colleagues silenced or punished for daring to challenge the decisions of senior managers in the past will not be in a hurry to volunteer for the role. They will need to be convinced first that candor really is valued; that their input, both positive and negative, is desired and will be acted on. The clearest signal they can receive is to see others rewarded for frank criticism. Again, it is not enough simply to tell people that the organization wants people to challenge the conventional wisdom and think for themselves. That can sound too much like lip service. But if people see others actually rewarded for that kind of thinking, they will understand that it really is what the company wants from them.

From the organization's point of view, it is worth rewarding such behavior because of the enormous benefits it can yield. Consultant Ram Charan sums up the value of candid, open—and decisive—dialogue as follows: "[It] allows tensions to surface and then resolves them by fully airing every relevant viewpoint. Because such dialogue is a process of intellectual inquiry rather than of advocacy, a search for truth rather than a contest, people feel emotionally committed to the outcome. The outcome seems 'right' because people have helped shape it. They are energized and ready to act."[13]

## The Role of Senior Managers

If criticism from employees at lower levels should be encouraged, senior managers considering others' proposals and ideas must also be free to criticize. After all, they are still the ones who have to ensure that strategy decisions are consistent with the company's overall direction, do not use up too many resources, and accurately reflect market conditions and the competitive situation.

The issue is, how and when and where should their criticisms be voiced? An informal dialogue is probably the least threatening context for expressing doubts or concerns. Maintaining a tone of honest truth seeking and respect for others' views and ideas is also important, as is systematically creating and encouraging opportunities for such dialogue.

### *Encouraging Independent Activity*

The story of how the inkjet printer was first conceived and then developed at Hewlett-Packard (HP) is both a prime example of the importance of allowing employees to engage in independent research and a cautionary tale about how companies can sometimes fail to empower employees to pursue their good ideas.

The initial idea of an inkjet printer arose during an informal discussion among a group of engineers working on a laser printer design; while standing in the hallway drinking coffee, they chatted casually about what kind of printer they would like to use themselves, and decided that a color inkjet printer with high resolution would be ideal. At the time, the idea was a pipe dream; inkjet printers were messy, unreliable, and terribly expensive.

Two of the engineers, however, began experimenting on their own with the concept, and after some trial and error came up with a rough prototype. But neither their manager nor their colleagues were enthusiastic, because the men themselves were not quite sure how—or why—it worked as well as it did. John Vaught, the prime mover behind the idea, was a self-taught engineer without a college degree, which made people even more suspicious of him. He was assigned to another project and told to stop working on his "unrealistic" inkjet printer venture. Only when the project manager he worked for left the firm abruptly did Vaught get some time again to devote to his idea; he then picked up some valuable supporters among senior people, who obtained funding for the project. As Vaught himself says, if they had gotten much further with the other project before the manager left, he might never have been able to return to his inkjet idea—which became one of the most profitable products the company had ever had.[14]

The question remains, how many such ideas never come to fruition because their initiators never experience the luck Vaught had when the project manager left? What can companies do to make sure that good ideas are heard and fostered? That is the other side of risk management: the risk that some potentially excellent and profitable ideas will die on the vine for lack of official encouragement and support.

In fact, although it was a near miss, it is not surprising that in the end Hewlett-Packard did get behind the inkjet printer. HP encourages its lab people to spend a lot of their time on independent, unofficial activities, and holds regular reviews to determine which projects to fund. It allows lab supplies to be used freely for such research, and explicitly expects its engineers to devote at least 10 percent of their time to it. At Toshiba, that figure is even higher: 15 percent. The channels are in place to review this type of research and determine which projects to fund. At many other companies, however, independent activity is not officially recognized or encouraged.

Finally, the decision on whether to support any specific

Apart from allowing employees time to develop their own ideas, steps that can be taken to encourage independent creativity, both inside and outside the lab context, include:

- Highlighting the role of such activity in internal publications that report on creative strategic innovations, in order to increase general awareness of its importance.
- Ensuring that this type of activity is widely reported on, rather than taking place in secret. Not only will that encourage others to pursue their own ideas, but it can lead to offers of help from people in different parts of the organization who may have something to offer a given project.

project should not rest with one manager alone. Multiple reviews make it more likely that the potential of an idea will not be missed. (This is another example of the paradox of empowerment: While approval processes for initiating research should not be cumbersome, the practice of multiple reviews—which may sound as though they will make it more difficult to get funding—actually work as a safeguard against a promising idea falling by the wayside.)

### Building a Participatory Culture

Regardless of the methods used to encourage wider participation, the success of these efforts will depend on a company culture that welcomes challenges to the status quo and encourages constructive debate. Again, it's not just a matter of paying lip service to those values; employees have to see them demonstrated by corporate leaders and actively fostered at all levels of the organization.

Perhaps the clearest message that an organization can send about its commitment to broader participation is to modify its systems as needed to promote and support this goal.

Systems for appraising performance, rewarding employees, training, and communication should encourage strategy making by every member of the business. In your company, are people below the management level trained, evaluated, and rewarded for their ability to think strategically or for their willingness to challenge conventional wisdom? Does the company culture welcome people who question what the organization does and why, or are they seen as troublemakers?

Many changes are required if the strategy-making process is truly to reflect the realities of the marketplace and become a source of competitive advantage. Wider involvement in the formal process is only one part of the picture. For companies to achieve timely responsiveness to their customers and their markets, they also need to find ways to capitalize on the informal, ad hoc ideas and activities that are bubbling up at all levels, as people interact with customers or pursue promising avenues of research. In the next chapter, we look at the kind of improvisational thinking—and doing—that can have future strategic implications, and how to tap into its potential.

## Key Points

- Skillful delegation is required for genuine empowerment. Responsibilities need to be clearly explained and the limits of people's discretion spelled out in advance. People should be consulted about just how much authority they need and want to carry out an assignment.

- Multilevel teams allow for input from people who work directly with customers, while speeding up the planning process by having people on board who can wield authority and influence.
- Not everyone in an organization can be directly involved in formulating key strategies, but soliciting broad input before the plan is finalized ensures that potential problems will be identified early, refinements can be made, and people will feel more committed to the final decision.
- Senior managers are responsible for encouraging and fostering independent activity among people throughout the organization.
- Reward and recognition systems and training and development programs need to reflect and reinforce the company's commitment to broader participation in strategy making.

# 4 | The Power of Improvisation

If you have ever watched a skilled troupe of actors taking part in an improvisation, you have seen a good example of how strategies evolve. Just as a business starts with a broad general strategy, an improvisational group usually starts with a loosely defined scenario. Let us say this group is four people in a waiting room. Then the moderator asks audience members for their suggestions: What are these people waiting for? Who are they? What is the relationship between them?

Depending on the audience's responses, the characters could become three pregnant women and one kangaroo waiting to see the doctor, or extraterrestrials applying for the U.S. space program, or hyperactive kids who have been summoned to the principal's office. The actors, masters of the art of emergence, may start with a few scripted lines. However, they soon take off from there and begin improvising their own lines, based on what has just been said. As in life, the endpoint is often unknown—it emerges out of people's creative responses to the audience's suggestions and what is happening on the stage.

In a similar way, effective companies are becoming more improvisational in their approach to strategy. For example, in the past, corporate strategy makers often developed a detailed, line-by-line script they intended the organization to follow. Planners determined the optimal approach to markets, the keys to keeping customers happy, and the ways to beat competitors. Such a scripted method may work in a traditional play on the stage—or in a more predictable business environment. In the current business world, however, customers respond, competitors innovate, and the situation changes before the script, or plan, can play itself out. Strategy makers, therefore, are becoming much less like playwrights and much more like improvisers. The script is increasingly based on audience input and the actors' own sense of what will work best.

A dictionary definition of "to improvise" is "to compose, or spontaneously compose and perform, on the spur of the moment and without any preparation." Yet in reality, successful improvisation is usually the product of years of training and experience that allow the actors to give a meaningful shape to their interactions and guide the plot to a satisfying conclusion. Not only do they choose a scenario that offers some interesting possibilities, they have some idea from their past work together how the others will respond. Each may have a favorite line or joke that he or she works in, regardless of the specific scenario. The group often has a fallback plan to rescue them if the scene begins to fall flat. They begin with a plan and a shared set of assumptions; their preparation, training, and experience give them the confidence to let the plan evolve. It is their knowledge of each other that enables the process of team improvisation to work, and it is the process that is key. Or, as Dwight D. Eisenhower said, "It's not the plan; it's the planning."

## Organizations as Improvisers

More and more, organizations are doing something similar to the actors described previously—paradoxically, they are planning ahead to allow strategies to emerge. That involves ensuring that new situations and new needs will be recognized and that their systems, processes, and culture will change as required to allow them to respond flexibly to new opportunities. They are learning to improvise, but within a structure.

In this case, the structure is provided by the organization's purpose and overall strategic direction, as well as a set of shared assumptions about goals and values. The common purpose and the shared view of the business bind people together and form the framework that allows meaningful strategies to emerge. The corporate actors are given a theme to improvise around—it could be one of the company's strategic goals, or a market whose potential seems worth exploring; they then focus their efforts around that theme but have the freedom to decide themselves how to approach it. Several groups might be given the same theme to work with and come up with wholly different scenarios.

---

As with the skilled troupe of actors, the success of improvisational strategy making relies on the skills of strategy makers at all levels of the organization—skills acquired through years of experience and training—and the ways in which they have learned to work together, based on their knowledge of each other's strengths.

---

Senior managers are encouraging the evolution of strategy in two key ways. First, as we have seen, they are delegating

73

decision-making authority to people at lower levels of the organization. As people feel more free to respond directly to customer needs, they make more and more decisions that may have strategic impact. In essence, they become on-the-spot improvisers, front-line strategists: experts on a specific customer, market, or process.

Second, companies are asking for more and more input from customers, gathered via surveys, customer forums, and joint planning sessions, as well as informal dialogue. Such real-time data provides an objective and thorough picture of changing customer needs and expectations—needs that can be addressed responsively only by allowing strategies to emerge through a process of improvisation.

Since my co-author and I first proposed this model of improvisational strategy making in an earlier book, *The New Strategists*, more and more companies have turned to improvisation to give them a competitive edge. Sun Microsystems is one organization that has grown and thrived by combining just such an improvisational approach, with plenty of customer input. For example, when Sun acquired a small British company that made computers for use in telecommunications, the unit assigned to manage the acquired business realized that it provided an opportunity to launch Sun more fully into the networking industry, a theme that top management had floated among the organization as a whole.

Knowing that it would be a matter of learning as they went along, they came up with a highly flexible implementation plan that evolved in response to market developments and the input of potential customers. Based on what customers told them they wanted, the project's leaders worked with the engineering and marketing people to design a product they felt could compete successfully, and even managed to develop it in roughly half the time such a process usually required. Having started with an inherited product that had never generated revenues of more than $25 million a year, the Sun group used what it had learned about customer requirements to design products that were bringing in more than $150 million just two years later. Thus, Sun became a central player in the market for converged network infrastructure.[1]

That kind of improvisational approach, however, can give rise to a number of challenges similar to the ones faced by the troupe of actors. These include: How do you train people to improvise? How can you be sure that the various different players will work well together? How do you make customers part of the improvisational process, rather than just information sources? What happens if things start going off the rails? And how can you be sure, once you start improvising, that you will wind up where you wanted to go?

## Improvisational Teamwork

Multifunctional or multilevel teams with representatives from the front lines can function like a group of improvising actors, working together to respond to audience suggestions and create a cohesive scenario. Salespeople are uniquely attuned to who is buying what and why, while customer and technical service reps know what problems customers are having with your products and services. Increasingly, these people are not only being asked to give their input into the formal strategy-making process, they are also encouraged to take the initiative to solve customers' current and potential problems on their own. Their actions then evolve into strategy.

As one expert on corporate creativity put it, "The employees on the front line tend to be the most creative, not because of who they are but because of where they are—dealing with customers, suppliers, and generally getting their hands dirty. What management is then called upon to do is channel that creativity in a way that contributes meaningfully to the bottom line."[2]

Savvy companies have begun to leverage the knowledge and insight of their front-line salespeople by making them part of cross-functional product development teams. Joann Smith, a principal at IBM Consulting Group's market-based innovation practice, puts it this way: "Because we are a 'service,' our salespeople are inextricably linked to the experience, and the experience is the product. Sales function involvement in product development efforts for a service organization is very important, because their interaction with an end customer is often part of the resulting offering itself."[3]

Carlos Cata, a former Kraft brand manager who is currently a group vice president of Frontera Foods, describes sales reps' involvement as "bringing a perspective on how to sell the product that will work in reality versus what we think will work at headquarters."[4] Wendy Ellis Gardner, a former brand manager at Quaker Oats, concurs, saying, "Participation of [front-line personnel] can prevent the [product development team] from making big mistakes at the shelf or the trade." One such mistake occurred when a major consumer products firm launched a product that was too large to fit on the shelves of one of its biggest distributors—a mistake that could easily have been avoided if account reps had been involved in the development process.[5]

Mike Morrow, a salesperson at SC Johnson, was part of a crossfunctional team assigned the task of developing a new product line. He led customer focus groups to uncover customer needs and participated in brainstorming sessions to generate new product ideas. In his view, "The big advantage [of my involvement] was molding ideas early in the new product development process. I was able to provide not only consumer insights, but also practical trade considerations, resulting in more realistic and sellable new product offerings."[6]

Indeed, as Southwest's legendary former CEO Herb Kelleher saw it, "Before you implement an idea that has been generated in the office, you should always take it to the field and ask for their criticisms. Pretty soon the idea will look like Swiss cheese—full of holes. They know what they're doing and we don't. They'll know right away, 'This won't work, that won't work, let me tell you why, this won't fit.' And they get it all right! 'You can do it, but not the way you talk about.' "[7]

In other words, rather than presenting people with a script that they must follow, they are presented with an idea and then allowed to tailor the script to the reality of what goes on. At Wal-Mart, Sam Walton's policy of allowing individual stores to improvise their own, differentiated strategies led to some of the most successful marketing initiatives in retailing history. Door greeters, blow-out sales, Moon Pie-eating contests and Oreo-stacking contests were all the brainchildren of Wal-Mart associates. "Sam Walton believed in an inverted pyramid with the associates in the store being the most important part of making the company successful," says Tom Coughlin, president and CEO of the Wal-Mart Stores division. "To me that just makes all kinds of sense." Store associates are at the top of the pyramid; the people at headquarters are there to support the associates in their job of taking care of customers.

At Wal-Mart, store managers have the authority to alter the product mix, while the chain's volume-producing-item (VPI) program allows every associate to participate in developing personalized displays within the store. As Coughlin says, "It is amazing what comes back from these associates on what we need to do. They understand better and are closer to the customer than we are, so they know what the customer wants."

In addition, it is company policy for buyers to include store associates in conference calls if they are considering a change associates will have the ultimate responsibility for implementing. Associates also attend the annual shareholders' meeting. "These people work in a variety of departments," explains Coughlin. "It is a fun time for them, and there are a lot of things that are done to make it exciting for them. We also take one full day and we have special seminars where we listen to them. [Management] is told to wear their ears and leave their tongues at home." Since these associates are the people closest to Wal-Mart's customers, "you are getting the very best advice that you can."[8]

By broadening the scope of delegation and spreading responsibility for taking meaningful action to a greater number of people, you are allowing for the emergence of strategy. As people have more freedom to work with customers to resolve problems and address needs, they generate more creative solutions. Those solutions, in turn, may form the kernel of future strategies.

However, this process can be challenging. For such an approach to succeed, the proper balance must be struck. People need to have a clear sense of the limits of their responsibility, as well as its scope; they need to be given a structure within which to improvise. (It is surprising how often the most improvisatory cultures are strongly grounded in operating efficiency, another example of how, paradoxically, freedom is only made possible by structure and order. Wal-Mart is a prime example of this.)

Of course, not every improvisation is going to succeed. Review processes need to be in place to ensure that mistakes are not perpetuated to the point where they turn into catastrophes. At the same time, it is important for people to understand that they will not be punished for honest mistakes. Any organization that wants to have a truly improvisatory culture will need to develop a much higher tolerance for failure than has traditionally been the norm. Mistakes need to be treated as learning opportunities rather than occasions for criticism and blame, which means focusing on the reasons behind them and encouraging people to explore ways to avoid similar problems in the future.

Wal-Mart's continuing success was partly predicated on this ability to learn from its mistakes, or to make use of whatever was positive about an overall negative experience. For example, although its original-format hypermarkets proved unsuccessful, they were the forerunners of its highly profitable chain of Wal-Mart supercenters, which combine in one setting a Wal-Mart store with a full-fledged grocery department. And while its Eco Stores have mostly gone out of business, the skylights and adjustable lighting systems they pioneered are now a feature of most new Wal-Marts.[9]

Many successful executives recount stories of learning valuable lessons from their mistakes, and of turning their individual learning into organizational learning. One such senior manager is Joe Sirianni, vice president of merchandising at the famed catalog retailer Lands' End. When asked to describe his biggest mistake ever, Sirianni recalled allowing 200,000 turtlenecks with faulty neckbands to be shipped to customers:

> We didn't discover until after they were shipped that the Lycra-and-cotton blend in the neck lost elasticity after several washes. We sent out 200,000 letters to the customers who had bought the faulty turtlenecks. About 45,000 responded, and we mailed them replacement turtlenecks. We also suspended sales of turtlenecks until we figured out what the heck we had on our hands. It turns

out that the fabric was not tested properly before it got to us. In the end we had to throw away about $1.5 million worth of turtlenecks. That taught me that even though you think a system is running properly, you can't let up on checking that it truly is.

Sirianni's lesson has become part of Lands' End policy:

> After that experience, we—along with our yarn supplier and knitter—put in more checks and balances to make sure faulty fabric never goes undetected again.[10]

## Two-Way Information Funnels

Another vital requirement for successful improvisation is having channels in place for funneling information back and forth between front-line strategists and senior management. Otherwise, there is no way of ensuring that improvisations will be aligned with overall strategic goals—or that successful improvisations will be capitalized on. After all, strategies have been evolving within organizations for as long as there have been organizations. But companies have not always been able to recognize them and incorporate them into their plans. What you need is a two-way communication system that both gives front-line decision makers all the information they require and disseminates the information they bring into the organization. Information sharing can take many forms, including the following:

- *Convene forums that give front-line people face-to-face access to formal strategy makers on a regular basis.* At Philips Electronics, employees present new ideas directly to a top executive committee for approval. "We're bringing top decision-makers to bear on new ideas so something terrific doesn't die on the vine," Executive Vice President Frank Carrubba says.[11]

Those involved in ongoing projects can also benefit greatly from access to senior people. Robert Silver, executive vice president of UBS Wealth Management USA, conducts periodic reviews of ongoing projects, where he asks his people what he can do—what barriers or roadblocks he can help them surmount—to help them achieve their goals. He also conducts quarterly town-hall meetings. In addition, he has launched a program of Breakfasts with Bob where "I meet twelve or so staff and talk about the business with them."[12]

Round tables are another effective venue for airing and developing front-line strategists' ideas. At Mt. Bachelor Ski and Summer Resort, for example, round tables are held every two weeks. President David Marsh, Ann Smith, vice president of human resources, and other senior executives meet with 6 to 10 employees from various departments and levels in an open forum. At one round table, the group was discussing how to make the season opening run more smoothly. Smith says: "One young woman made a suggestion about our ticketing system. We're all sitting there thinking, 'Oh, yeah—that's so obvious.' But we never thought of it because we're not out there on the front lines actually handling it."

- *Set up formal, ongoing suggestion systems.* Any company that genuinely hopes to take advantage of employee knowledge and insight requirements will need to do much more than install a traditional suggestion box (described by management expert Karen Cates as "a black hole").[13] People need to know both that management is seriously committed to the program, and that they will be rewarded for their good ideas.

At Cleco Power LLC, a division of the Cleco Corporation, the Ideas for Excellence program offers employees a 5 percent cash reward, up to a maximum of $5,000, for suggestions that lead to quantifiable savings. More than 1,700 suggestions have been submitted since the program was launched in 1999, and 230 of them have been implemented. One that led to significant savings was a suggestion by Clark Bordelon, a senior engineering project coordinator, that the company use an empty fuel tank already onsite to meet its need for additional storage space: The company saved $350,000 by acting on this idea rather than building additional facilities. Another innovative idea—providing glow-in-the-dark magnets for power outages—made electrical emergencies less traumatic for customers.[14]

Similarly, the U.K. retailer Asda has a suggestion program whereby its employees gain points that can be redeemed for either cash or gifts if their ideas are implemented. More than 1,000 suggestions are submitted by employees each month to the program (which goes by the name Tell Archie, a reference to Asda's chief executive, Archie Norman, to emphasize that top management is listening).[15]

In 1997, Union Pacific introduced Idea Works, a formal employee feedback program that feeds all employee suggestions into the organization's systems for strategy evaluation. As with the Tell Archie program, any individual employee or team whose idea is implemented is awarded points that can be redeemed for their choice of travel or merchandise. Says Paul Richardson, account executive for Carlson Marketing Group, which guided Union Pacific in its introduction of the program, "Part of the IdeaWorks process is to encourage employees to think like business owners and develop a good business case for their suggestions."

At the railroad's Salt Lake City office, one team that included employees involved in daily track repairs came up with a suggestion that saved the company $470,000 by making the process of replacing broken bolts much more efficient, and less damaging to track parts. In another division, an employee from the freight car repair shop suggested the use of a paint that was both easier to apply and more ecologically sound. Both the company's profits and the environment benefited.[16]

One company that devised an especially innovative suggestion system was the First Maryland Bancorp (now Allfirst Financial), whose Brainstorm program was designed to last just 12 weeks; the committees formed to review employee suggestions were asked to decide on them within 7 days of submission. Employees were encouraged to form teams to come up with ideas for increasing revenues or decreasing expenses, and to provide detailed cost–benefit analyses supporting their proposals.

To help ensure the success of the effort, program coordinators, leaders of suggestion teams, and members of the suggestion evaluation committee were all given special training, and CEO Charles W. Cole recorded a personal video message to communicate his commitment and enthusiasm to all the bank's employees. He also participated in numerous meetings to introduce the effort. Finally, rewards were promised to employees whose suggestions were adopted. (Of the $3 million or so that the program wound up costing, $2 million was spent on rewards.)

Some of the suggestions adopted involved more efficient ways to route telecommunications circuits, stopping the distribution of large computer-generated reports to employees who no longer needed them, and reducing maintenance costs on computer equipment at branch banks. The savings achieved were almost eight times the cost of Brainstorm. According to Senior Vice President Brian King, the benefits went way beyond the program's initial payoff. By teaching employees the cost of doing business, and making them more aware of the bottom line, it enabled them to make better ongoing decisions about the allocation of resources. It also fired up their creativity and entrepreneurial spirit.[17]

■ *Provide frequent and informal access to management by encouraging encounters between people from all levels of the company.* Company practices that segregate senior managers from employees by isolating their workspaces (the executive floor) and gathering places (the executive lunchroom) can prevent good ideas from making it through the class barrier. That is why a participating member of IdeasUK (the Association of Suggestion Schemes) started a tradition known as Donuts with Dave: the chief executive opens his office on certain days to everyone *but* senior management, so that employees can just walk in and have their ideas listened to by the head of the organization.[18]

A similar program is in operation at Body Shop, also in the United Kingdom, where every employee has the ear of top management through what's known as the DODGI (the Department of Damn Good Ideas). Employees who call this line with an idea are put through to a member of senior management, who discusses it with them.

At Sun Microsystems, such access to top executives is an ongoing policy. For instance, John, an M.B.A. student who worked as a summer intern at Sun, was concerned that the company was not dealing with issues of Internet regulation on a timely enough basis. He decided that an Internet Regulation Rapid Response Team was needed to help it take advantage of opportunities—and forestall emergencies—that might arise in the future.

John submitted a proposal for such a team to his immediate superiors, and then sent it to Alan Baratz, president of JavaSoft. "Then I called his office and set up a time to meet with him.

What I did is like a student intern in a General Motors marketing department calling the president of the Buick division for a meeting. The Public Policy director and I met with Baratz and his PR person. He agreed to go ahead with my plan." In the end, John, who had come on board as a lowly intern, was asked to stay on and lead the team he had launched.

- *Ensure that formal systems are in place for reviewing and evaluating independent, potentially fruitful projects and activities on a regular basis.* We saw in Chapter Three that both Hewlett-Packard and Toshiba expect their people to engage in independent research and have regular reviews of their projects. The same expectations and processes exist at IBM Research, where researchers submit project descriptions annually; these descriptions outline current work they are doing outside the scope of the division's formal projects.

At Asea Brown Boveri (ABB)'s R&D operation in Raleigh, North Carolina, an open contest is held at intervals throughout the year. Anyone can submit an innovative technology idea in the areas—software engineering, industrial IT, manufacturing technology and robotics, and electric and alternative power systems—in which ABB specializes. Panels comprised of experts in the different categories then review each idea submitted. Since the program's inception in 1999, more than 15 ideas submitted to the contest have led to major projects and new business for ABB. In 2000 alone, 130 ideas were generated, of which 30 were funded.[19]

It can be equally productive and useful to employ such practices outside the scientific labs. At Coca-Cola's innovation centers, employees brainstorm ideas for new beverages and new packaging. After review by management, partnerships are created with other local business units to turn the most viable concepts generated in these idea laboratories into reality.[20]

Making sure senior people are kept in touch with the improvisational work being done by teams and individuals within the organization increases the likelihood that formal planning processes will take evolving market trends into account and incorporate emerging strategies. Such an information-sharing process is most effective when accompanied by corresponding methods for keeping people updated on how their input is being used and by recognition and compensation systems that reward people for providing such information.

Yet while front-line people within the company are a critical link in the communications chain with your customers and markets, they are still essentially translators. Increasingly, companies are exploring even more direct ways of getting customers involved in the strategy-making process, which in turn suggests the need for further improvisational responses.

## Getting Customer Input

Organizations use a variety of ways to gather feedback from customers and other external stakeholders. Some companies circulate draft strategic plans not only to employees but also to key suppliers for their suggestions. They may also conduct customer focus groups and forums during which they share plans for their future technical direction with customers, and customers explain their own long-term plans and expectations. Strategies can then be adjusted accordingly.

When Kenwood launched an initiative to be first-to-market with a series of new consumer electronic products, it began by soliciting input from its dealers. It was dealers, for example, who suggested the enhancements that the company implemented to its Sovereign line of home entertainment products. Based on their recommendations, the PowerTouch remote, a wireless, infrared LCD touch-panel remote that Kenwood has sold for several years, now has an interface that allows installers to customize it according to their different needs.[21]

When the Cordis Corporation, a Florida manufacturer of medical devices, launched an initiative in 1993 to increase its share of the market for angioplasty balloons (used to open the blocked arteries of cardiac patients), the company interviewed cardiologists, nurses, and laboratory personnel. It then used the insights it gained to lay the foundation for a whole new product strategy that addressed unsatisfied needs in new market segments. Cordis also decided, based on what the interviewees told them, that some of the products it had under development were not going to be a hit in the marketplace, so they suspended costly further work on them—a good example of how flexibility around strategy can be key to success.

While Cordis had set itself a relatively modest goal of increasing its market share (then 1 percent of the angioplasty balloon market) by just 5 percent, it actually gained a market leadership position. That was only the beginning. By listening to its potential customers, it identified a need for a device that could be placed in a treated artery to prevent recurrent blockage. Cordis developed this product, now called a *stent*, which became the fastest-growing product in medical device history, producing nearly $1 billion in revenue in its first year.[22]

Stryker Instruments in Kalamazoo, Michigan is also a manufacturer of medical devices: powered surgical instruments and related accessories for orthopedic and neuro- and spinal-surgery procedures. Stryker encourages all its 600 employees to visit hospitals to observe the use of the devices it provides. "To see the [instruments] that you have built in action on a human being is eventful," says Nina Hickok, senior technician/ team supervisor and an 11-year veteran at Stryker.

Curt Hartman, Stryker's vice president and general manager, notes, "About 70 percent of the reps' workweek is spent in the O.R., because that's where it happens. The surgeon, the orthopedic tech, the spine tech, and the neuro tech are using the products and giving us feedback: 'This works well. This doesn't work well. If I could do this it would make this procedure faster.'"

"With close customer contact, you're not trying to develop a product, you're trying to develop a solution for the customer," says Lonny Carpenter, vice president of operations. As a result, Stryker Instruments' products continually become more user friendly. It overhauled its bone-cement mixing system, for example, in response to surgeons' complaints that the existing system was messy, created air bubbles, was difficult to mix and distribute, and had an unpleasant odor. The new system has a mixing bowl whose lock-down lid and charcoal filter eliminate almost all the fumes.

Like Stryker, Compaq's emphasis on creating user-friendly products has led it to involve customers directly in its development process. For example, when the company undertook to create storage space for compact discs within its computers' central processing unit (CPU), internal evaluators were unanimously approving of what the designer came up with, a CPU with a pouch on the side. Customers, however, were not so enthusiastic. They felt the pouch was unattractive, so Compaq went back and changed the design to hide the pouch.[23]

### Customer Surveys

Perhaps the most common means for gathering customer input is the customer survey. When used in conjunction with the internal information funnel (not *instead* of it), surveys can provide valuable insight into customer needs. Before beginning the design process for major new products, Compaq surveys thousands of users via the Web, as well as soliciting their input in focus groups and at trade shows. In fact, "Our customers play an important role by telling us what products they would like us to design and the feature functionality they desire."[24]

Even more sweeping than product development was the customer feedback that recently led Cisco Systems to restructure its entire operations. Its new organizational structure, aligned around 11 technology groups, is a direct response to customer demand for "a network of networks"—a seamless way of transparently integrating solutions across extranets, intranets, and the Internet.[25]

The Ohio Casualty Group (OCG), a respected property and casualty insurer, has invested a lot of time, thought, and effort in creating what it calls a "customer-intimate" organization. It prides itself on listening to the voice of the customer. That means its business strategies directly reflect the feedback it systematically solicits from both agents and customers. As Bill Minor, senior vice president and director of marketing, describes it:

> We study and digest our findings, then develop programs that meet the needs and desires our research has identified.

The company's key tool is a customer relations assessment study. Minor explains:

> We use this device to build a bond with our policyholders and assess how we're doing. . . . We focus on so-called 'moments of truth': policyholders' perceptions of our billing, policy delivery, loss control, and claims service, as well as agent contact.

After conducting this assessment, Minor says:

We take each of these areas and statistically link it back to the pol-icyholder's level of commitment to determine what areas have the greatest impact on the policyholder's relationship with OCG. We ask the same questions of customers of other insurers to measure their service against ours. This research effort is ongoing and al-ways evolving. We strive for immediate feedback so we can de-velop responsive action programs."[26]

## *Designing the Optimal Process*

Apart from the *what* of customer feedback, you might also want to have an ongoing dialogue about the *how* of it. That means encouraging input about the practices used to gather feedback from customers, and the ways in which it is used. Do customers feel that their needs and concerns have been ad-dressed, and that the time they spent providing feedback has been worth it? A team might be assigned to evaluate the process on an ongoing basis, and to talk to customers about how it could be improved.

When British Airways (BA) found that some of its cus-tomers felt thwarted in their efforts to register their concerns with the company, they overhauled their processes for ensur-ing that customer views would be heard. First, they estab-lished more than a dozen Listening Posts where customers can air their complaints. Then they designed an international free-post comment card to make sure people would not need to find stamps in foreign countries.

The airline also launched Customer Listening Forums be-tween BA executives and customers, where grievances are aired in person, and introduced a Fly-with-Me program: Customer relations people and BA executives actually accompany customers on their trips in order to experience typical problems firsthand. Finally, BA developed a Recovery Point program that allows front-line staff access to recovery resources and ensures that customer complaints are fed into the company's database.

BA continually monitors its successes and failures in solving particular service issues. It analyzes every aspect of the recovery process and researches customer likes and dislikes concerning customer relations' responses and recovery efforts. For instance, in a recent survey on complaint handling, customers complained about the airway's lengthy and protracted "adjudication" process; this led BA to streamline the process.[27]

### Sorting or Crunching the Information

However you gather the information, the most important thing is what you do with it. Make sure that it can be sorted or crunched in a variety of ways. You may want to have breakdowns of data for specific units, functions, products, or locations. Then be sure to feed the data back to everyone in the organization. You should let people in the regional offices know what their customers think of the service they provide, and give distribution feedback on how well it is satisfying customers.

You should also set targets for improvement, determining what the most important areas for focus over the next year should be; what rating you want customers to give you in this area a year from now; and how you are going to reach that target. In the process of answering such questions and implementing the improvements, new strategies are likely to emerge. Most important, these strategies will be based on an accurate reading of customers' needs, not on internal guesswork.

Once targets have been set, it is important to allow the strategies for reaching them to evolve. The targets provide the goal, the structure. Reaching the goal will require improvisation, as people in the organization discover what works and what does not. Encouraging such an improvisational climate is one of the leader's most important roles.

## Building an Improvisational Culture

Effective leaders make sure that systems like the ones we have described are in place to encourage the emergence of new strategies. Lars Kolind, former CEO of the highly successful Danish hearing aid manufacturer Oticon, describes the leader's role as follows: "I don't see myself as a captain who steers the ship. I see myself as a naval architect who designs the ship. . . . It is more important to design the organization to act in a clever and responsible way than to control every action."

Building a culture that is comfortable with improvisation is about more than systems, however; it is about a mindset that celebrates creative responses, that looks at changing circumstances as opportunities rather than annoyances. Such an attitude needs to be modeled by the organization's leaders in order for evolving strategies to be valued and used. Kolind practiced such flexibility: "As opportunities emerged, we saw them and we acted. Although Oticon had a budget and a strategic plan, we didn't take them very seriously. We looked at long-term and short-term opportunities in a much more organic and dynamic way."[28]

Amar Bhide, a management writer, eloquently summarizes the assumptions behind this critical leadership philosophy:

"Businesses characterized by ease of entry, fast action, and service intensity are like poker, not chess. You play each hand as it is dealt and quickly vary tactics to suit conditions."[29]

In short, then, leaders need to provide a structure that fosters improvisation and enables strategies to emerge. They also need to serve as role models by demonstrating flexibility in their own behavior and by focusing on creating value for customers. However, while their role is significant, many others in the organization will also need to play a role in the emergent strategy-making process. In Part II, we explore a context for thinking about the current strategic state of your organization, and for determining what types of strategies are required going forward. We also look at the skills and the types of knowledge that equip people at different levels to be successful strategy makers, the support they will need from the organization itself—and the dilemmas and challenges they will face.

## Key Points

- Organizations need to learn how to plan for strategies to emerge—how to improvise within a structure. That structure is provided by the business's overall goals.
- Cross-functional teams made up of different types of people in direct contact with customers can be a fertile source of exciting new ideas.
- Encouraging a climate of improvisation entails developing a tolerance for failure; otherwise, people will be reluctant to take risks. Companies that can learn from their mistakes are some of the most successful businesses in history.
- Two-way information funnels are needed, to allow ideas to pass back and forth between different levels of the company. People on the front lines need the authority to

respond to customers on their own, and access to senior managers who can okay ideas that go beyond the scope of the front liner's own activities. They also need to be rewarded for ideas that work.

- Whenever possible, customers themselves should be made part of the strategy-making process; their views can be learned either through surveys or through other means of information gathering.

# II | The Individual Strategy Maker

# 5 | Thinking like a Strategist

*For the system to work, every person in the company has to be-
come a well-rounded generalist who understands all aspects of our
operation, who understands the economy in which we work, and
who has the good of the whole company in mind when he or she
makes decisions. It's like every [employee in my corporation] is a
mini-CEO.*

—Roger Sant, Chairman, AES Corporation[1]

Arriving at inclusive strategies will require empowerment, improvisation, and broader involvement, but it also calls for something more than that: making sure that everyone involved is able
to think like a strategist. That is, people at all levels of the organization must be able to consider their daily actions in terms of
how they will affect the business's ability to compete more effectively over the long term.

Traditionally, this has entailed making decisions that are
consistent with the organization's strategies, but people also have
to understand when the strategies themselves need to evolve in

response to changes and potential changes in the marketplace. In fact, strategic thinking is very similar to systems thinking, an approach popularized by Peter Senge in *The Fifth Discipline*. At its core, systems thinking involves seeing the interconnected nature of things—how one part affects and is affected by others, and the need for each person's actions and decisions to be shaped by a sense of the whole.

## The Four Strategic States

In the course of the strategy work we have done with diverse types of companies over the past 20 years, my colleagues and I have come to appreciate that every organization is different, and no two situations will ever be completely alike. At the same time, however, we have learned to recognize certain archetypal "strategic states" that seem to codify and exemplify the different possible situations organizations face.

Keep in mind, however, that the definitions that follow—and the challenges described—should not be seen as a rigid system of classification, or an attempt to prescribe specific actions. Instead, they are a way to clarify and focus the issues involved in a particular situation to help people make the best possible decisions about what needs to be done. They offer a way of thinking about what a business is doing strategically in fairly straightforward terms that are directly related to day-to-day experience.

If, for example, your company's strategy is to maintain its current market share, your job and your goals and your way of thinking about the business will be shaped by that fact; if your company's strategy is to develop a new product line, that becomes the determining factor.

---

### The Four Strategic States

- *Fort state.* We are an established business; our focus is on maintaining or improving on our current position.
- *Eagle state.* We are creating a new business, product, market, or industry.
- *Slim Down state.* We are slimming down by trimming our product lines, production facilities, distribution systems, or markets served.
- *Circled Wagons state.* We are currently in a crisis, and are fighting for the survival of our business.

---

Maybe you knew immediately, as you read these descriptions, which state your business was in—while some efforts and projects might not fit neatly, maybe it is clear that, by and large, it is in an Eagle or a Fort or a Circled Wagons state. But it is also possible that it is pursuing strategies in two, three, or even four of the categories. If so, it is not unique. In our consulting business, when we ask the executives we work with to identify their units' current strategies, they often report a smorgasbord of activities reflecting two or three strategic states. A business may be rationalizing its old product lines, introducing new ones, and reengineering a key work process.

Unfortunately, while some of these activities may be strictly necessary, it is very difficult to maintain strategic focus while pursuing such diverse strategies. It is also difficult for people to make their own decisions when the strategic focus is unclear to them. If for example, they are confused about whether they should be concentrating on developing new products or on phasing out unprofitable old ones, they will not know where to invest their time, money, and energy.

When people are unsure about which of the competing strategies reflects the overall direction of the business, they usually pursue the ones they are most comfortable with, and the comfort level tends to be higher with strategies that do not entail significant change or significant risk. That means innovation or bold new initiatives are less likely when people are uncertain about what strategic state their business is in.

Of course, the organization as a whole may contain business units in different strategic states. If coordination is handled well, and a unifying vision exists, the organization should still be able to retain its overall focus. But an individual business unit is unlikely to be able to formulate and implement strategies effectively if it does not have a clearly defined strategic focus. It is this focus that will determine how it addresses its markets and competitors, and how it allocates its resources.

## Principles for Strategic Thinking

### Fort

A Fort business usually boasts a leadership or strong position in its industry. The word "Fort" comes from the Sanskrit word meaning "to strengthen or elevate." Companies that follow Fort strategies do exactly that—they strengthen their existing organizations to elevate their market position over that of their competitors.

A wide variety of business strategies may be used to feed and maintain a Fort and to keep a company, business, or function in this strong strategic state. The most dramatic (and highest-risk) strategy for a Fort is market penetration—that is, attacking another Fort. Companies pursuing this strategy do not always intend to start a market war; however, a war frequently emerges and intensifies as positions are threatened. The market war between Coca-Cola and Pepsi for leadership in the soft drink industry provides a prime example of Forts at war.

Forts also pursue strategies designed to maintain market share position, grow with industry volume, and achieve operational excellence. They may choose to solidify their positions through emphasis on technological breakthroughs in process capabilities, or by licensing products or processes or developing new markets.

It is important to note that all Fort strategies involve active efforts to maintain, improve, and strengthen market position. A strong business must never become merely a cash cow; too many businesses have been milked to death by complacency and by the assumption that they will stay on top of the industry by simply doing what they have done in the past. Maintaining and improving on a strong position in any industry requires constant attention to strategic action.

Despite the military overtones of the word, a Fort need not be run by a single general, with foot soldiers obediently carrying out his commands. However, the concept of defending a Fort is a necessary part of the strategic principles that work best for this type of business. Those principles include the following:

*Clarify the Goal: To Maintain or to Gain?*   As noted above, the key decision for a Fort, the one that should always drive the choice of specific strategies, is whether to maintain current position or go for further penetration of the market. Maintaining position means growing at the same pace as the market, and therefore keeping the same percentage of market share you have now. Market penetration means capturing a larger share of the market from your competitors.

But maintaining your current position does not equal stagnation. If you are a leader in your industry, or if it is enjoying rapid growth, maintaining share is a monumental task in itself, as Intel discovered during its long-running struggle with arch-rival AMD. You will need to pursue excellence, a high degree of innovation, and continuing improvement of your product line and services; you will also need to differentiate yourself from your competitors and pay constant attention to market-ing. As a Fort, you will be perpetually in danger of being at-tacked by both other entrenched competitors and new entrants into your territory.

*Market penetration.* Increasing your current market share is usually achieved by manipulating the marketing mix: lowering prices, increasing the value of products and services, advertising more aggressively. When Ford Motor Company's Alex Trotman said, "We are going to be the world's leading auto company," he was essentially announcing a market penetration strategy against GM, Fiat, Volkswagen, Toyota, and Nissan.

Market penetration is the equivalent of declaring war, and the risks are always high. The strategy may be used offensively or in response to an attack by others, when you have no choice but to strike back. But even if your strategy is to maintain position, a competitor's aggressive attempt to take some of your market share may draw you into a market war you never really wanted. Market wars pit one Fort against another and will require all your resources until your strategic goals are achieved or the strat-egy is abandoned.

As the airline industry discovered in the 1990s, market wars can prove detrimental to the industry overall, lowering profit margins for all competitors. While many people see market pen-etration as the most attractive and proactive strategy, it is always dangerous and expensive, and should never be embarked on without very careful consideration of the risks.

*Do It Best.*   Whether you are trying to maintain market share or to gain it, you must surpass your competitors in some critical areas in order to succeed. Learning to do it best requires just that—learning. This means, in a nutshell, using experience to help guide the work of the organization in the future. Learning from experience is a key asset of the successful Fort organization. Somewhere in the organization, people have "seen it, done it, been there." So they have lessons to share with others.

At the same time, organizations cannot rely on past experience alone. A Fort's ability to maintain or grow its market share also depends on the ability of people in the business to acquire and use new knowledge and skills, or, very simply, to become continuous learners. Alvin Toffler, in his book *Future Shock*, talks about a survival kit for the future. He ranks "knowing how to learn" as one of the highest-priority skills. It was also at the top of the American Society for Training and Development's list of the most important workplace skills in a recent survey of the top corporations in the United States.

---

Unfortunately, Forts have not always created a positive learning environment. Too often they reward and encourage routine, play-it-safe responses within a fear-of-failure climate that encourages survival behavior rather than proactive learning.

---

Leaders at all levels have a dual role to play in enhancing organizational learning. First, they have to be learners themselves. As the renowned spiritual leader J. Khrishnamurti wrote, "Learning is the very essence of humility, learning from everything and everybody. There is no hierarchy in learning."

Leaders must also serve as teachers, becoming involved in the development of others through informal and formal mentoring, coaching, facilitating, and so on. The legendary Jack Welch not only served as a teacher to thousands of GE employees by modeling the kinds of behavior—courageous, committed, commonsensical—that he wanted from others. He also personally conducted training sessions for employees once a month.

Thomas Tierney, worldwide managing director of the consulting firm Bain & Company, describes his vision for the company as "a global community of 'teacher-learners.' " Tierney is the leading advocate for shaping and articulating Bain's learning vision, which, in his words, is to "create the best environment in the world and learn how to add value to businesses." To achieve this vision, Bain enlists its best consultants to teach at the internal Bain Academy, where the "outside-in" approach to learning that is at the core of its consulting practice is also applied.[2]

It is the senior leaders who set up the formal systems that encourage people to learn, including training and development systems, job rotations, ongoing improvement efforts, and feedback systems. But people at all levels can coach each other informally, and can and should be giving each other feedback. It is important for everyone in the organization to understand that the purpose of feedback is to be helpful—to both the individual receiving it and the organization as a whole. Given in that spirit, feedback is a key tool in ensuring that an established Fort organization continues to learn, grow, and evolve.

*Replace Yourself.* Effective Fort organizations do not hesitate to develop new products and services, even if they will threaten existing lines of business. Some have called this practice "eating your lunch before someone else eats it for you." Hewlett-Packard, for example, is well known for its willingness to replace its own products. HP's laser printers compete against its own line of cheaper inkjet printers, and the inkjet models are steadily taking market share away from the more expensive ones. HP's former CEO Lew Platt put it this way: "We have to be willing to cannibalize what we're doing today in order to ensure our leadership in the future. It's counter to human nature, but you have to kill your business while it is still working."[3]

IBM's top executives were notoriously *un*willing to cannibalize their mainframe computer business, which meant they failed to take timely advantage of the PC revolution. Belatedly, they realized their error, but playing catch-up is tough in the computer industry. As late as 1994, IBM was still generating too great a percentage of its revenues from the mainframe business. It took Lou Gerstner, an outsider, to refocus the business on software and services.

In essence, Forts renew themselves by launching new businesses—thus becoming Eagles. The Fort's resources are used to develop the Eagle businesses, which, if they are successful, eventually become Forts in their own right. That is what happened with Eastman Kodak's digital photography product line—once an Eagle venture for the company, digital cameras are now a Fort unto themselves. The strategic challenge is to manage the two kinds of business separately and to find ways, despite this separation, to coordinate their efforts when both can benefit.

DuPont's comprehensive business initiative framework is an interesting attempt to launch new businesses from a Fort. The framework provides for innovation at the development stage while also leveraging some of the management processes and practices that have contributed to DuPont's success. It involves a small, multifunctional development team and a work flow concept that calls for developing only those deliverables that are required for informed decision making at that stage of the process. (A list of potential partners is drawn up early on, for example, but a choice is not made until much later.) The idea is to ensure that the team stays focused on what is important right at that moment, while not becoming rigid or losing creativity. At the end of each phase, a structured decision-making meeting is held, and senior management decides whether and where to allocate more resources to the project.

It may be too soon to tell how successful the framework will be over the long term, but it has already yielded impressive results in several cases. Among them is a joint venture with the Taiwanese Far Eastern Textile Company: a $100 million nylon fiber plant, constructed by FETC in Taiwan, using new fiber-spinning technology from DuPont.[4]

### Eagle

An Eagle establishes its nest in a defensible area and increases the size of that nest year after year. If it has a distinct competitive advantage, is well run and pursues sound strategies, it will, as noted earlier, eventually become a Fort. (Microsoft is a perfect example.)

An Eagle is keen–sighted, strong, and fearless; it attacks prey that can be overwhelmed swiftly and without warning. Like its namesake, a business in this state is looking for opportunities that have previously gone unnoticed or have been unavailable. Eagle strategies are used to manage the creation of a new business, product, or market—new to the company, if not to the world as a whole. These strategies include forward integration, creation of excess capacity to meet future growth, and the development of a new foreign business.

When Bentley, for example, decided to introduce a new,

more moderately priced vehicle into its U.S. markets, it had to come up with a new marketing strategy. Traditionally, the company had used micromarket prospecting tactics to generate sales leads. Potential European clients might be invited to the legendary Le Mans auto race, where they could sip champagne and smoke cigars while watching the Bentley racing car speed around the track. Obviously, this was not a strategy to be adopted when trying to sell less expensive cars to Americans.

Instead, Bentley identified ZIP codes that were home to its affluent target demographic. It then got involved with local charities in those regions in order to meet likely customers for its new vehicle. It also began sponsoring its own driving events—top-of-the-line, five star-resort road trips—and made its presence known at 20 U.S. racetrack events in 2000. "We have people at all these kinds of events, showing cars if possible, and explaining the brand," says Alasdair Stewart, president and chief executive officer of Bentley Motors, the American arm of Bentley. "From there, we set up mailing lists and develop one-to-one relationships before directing leads to dealerships." Bentley is thereby able to retain its mystique while cultivating new customer relationships.[5]

Of course, Eagles can also be entirely new companies. In either case, startup businesses work best when they are run differently from more established ones. Here are some key principles:

*Keep the Eagles Out of the Fort.* Businesses or functions in a startup mode need plenty of autonomy and freedom to find new opportunities. Trying to fly an Eagle as though you were defending a Fort is almost always a mistake. "Those red-tape antibodies come up and try to snuff you out," one manager who was struggling to run a new venture housed within an established business remarked.

*Do Not Declare War on a Fort.*    In the vast majority of cases, Forts have more resources at their command than less-established Eagle businesses. When an Eagle attacks a Fort, the Fort will invariably fight back, and thanks to its superior resources, it is likely to win. For instance, when tiny startup Transmeta went to war on Intel with its launch of Crusoe, a fast, energy-efficient microprocessor for mininotebooks, Intel launched an all-out counterattack, taking advantage of its ultralow-voltage technology to develop a still faster processor that used even less energy.[6] The result was that Transmeta's high-flying Eagle, which had been the darling of many industry analysts and journalists, was shot down in midair. Having been hailed as "threatening to break the Windows and Intel grip on the personal-computer industry,"[7] Transmeta found itself, a scant year later, laying off 40 percent of its workers after posting losses of $37.5 million on sales of $7.5 million.[8]

Transmeta's strategic mistake is not uncommon. Borland, an upstart in the software industry, had started an aggressive price war with its Fort competitors just a few years earlier, and had been beaten at its own game by Microsoft. Similarly, Informix Software, a brash young software company, went up against its rival Oracle (the number one database vendor in the market) with a new object-relational model. Oracle was not about to be vanquished. It launched a ruthless two-pronged counterattack. First, it hired 11 of Informix's key programmers; then, it gave them the task of developing another version of the technology. Informix had also underestimated how successful Microsoft's Windows NT OS would be in the database arena. The company saw its stock plummet and eventually go under.[9] As a competitor of Transmeta remarked of its lopsided war against Intel, "It is never easy to depose a king."[10]

---

Instead of trying to depose a king, the most successful Eagles find a unique niche and steer clear of the king's armies for as long as possible. Eventually, if a business is successful, it will grow into an established Fort and compete against other Forts. The timing of this shift is critical. Cocky Eagle businesses, fresh from a string of successes, can easily misjudge the power of their industries' leaders and head directly for strategic disaster.

---

*Get Yourself Some Risk Takers.* People who work in businesses in the Eagle state must be prepared to deal with unknowns and accept high risk. They will also require creativity, flexibility, and the ability to handle problems independently.

Too often, people are chosen to lead startup businesses based on a strong track record in more established operations. Unfortunately, their skills and strengths may actually be liabilities in their new situation. For example, one large manufacturing conglomerate launched an electronics component business based on a new technology that allowed them to make silicon wafers for integrated circuits at about half the cost of the traditional technology. The business seemed to have vast potential, but just as it was taking off, the general manager left. His replacement, who had been very successful in one of the company's established businesses, tried to manage the Eagle as though it were a Fort. He introduced more systematic—but also more cumbersome— policies and procedures, and brought in other senior managers who were used to managing Fort enterprises, because they were the sort of people with whom he felt comfortable. The business stalled. Later, it was sold for a fraction of what it might have been worth.

Of course, people's management styles and approaches can change. Furthermore, research has shown that providing leaders with new types of job challenges is often instrumental to their development. However, many people find it very hard to manage the transition. When you are choosing staff for a new business, it is important to make sure they are comfortable operating in that kind of environment.

### Slim Down

Not every business achieves the ideal of the Eagle that becomes a Fort and then spins off Eagles. Without continual improvement, a Fort can easily become fat. The growth of the existing organization may have slowed or stopped, while the Fort systems, structure, and staffing have outlived their usefulness.

A business in a Slim Down state needs to diet. Usually, as with an individual dieter, that is because it failed to maintain good habits, did not monitor itself carefully enough, or did not make the adjustment required to stay trim. That is what happened with Levi Strauss. In 1996, their sales stood at $7.1 billion. By 2001, that figure had declined to about $3 billion—a result of treating jeans as a commodity and neglecting fashion and trends.

The need for Slim Down strategies can also be triggered by industry conditions that no longer allow for adequate returns. In the 1970s, when oil companies and resource-rich countries moved into chemical production, leaving existing producers with overbuilt capacity, the entire chemical industry had to slim down. They undertook major rationalizations of plants and products. In the mid-1980s, the pendulum began to swing the other way; capacity could not keep up with demand, and the chemical Forts enjoyed a tremendous boom. The late 1980s and early 1990s saw another major shift. The cycle continues.

Slim Down strategies include rationalizing the company's product line, production, distribution, or markets. Levi's has gone from 51 to 8 plants; Ford, also facing declining sales and profits after several years of less than compelling product lines, along with reliability and quality problems that have resulted in extensive bad press, has plans to cut 35,000 jobs worldwide, close 5 plants, and slash production by 16 percent. In an extreme case, a company in a Slim Down state may opt for the strategy of paring back to its "little jewel"—the organization's most profitable piece.

Here are some key principles to follow should you find yourself in a Slim Down state:

*Do It Fast; Get It Done.*   Those companies that react to new threats by slimming down swiftly and compassionately often emerge as the healthiest and most vigorous competitors in their industries. In many companies, however, ground is conceded grudgingly and at considerable expense. When the need for Slim Down strategies is not identified early and communicated effectively, the Slim Down state can become debilitating. That is a lesson Pan Am learned the hard way. For the last 10 or 15 years of its existence, it failed to acknowledge its manifold problems—excess capacity, numerous operating inefficiencies—and therefore never reconfigured its assets to properly align with the marketplace. Instead, it cannibalized itself, until it was finally forced into bankruptcy, ending a long and proud history.

Conversely, however, as with a diet that is taken to extremes, the health of a business can be compromised if Slim Down strategies are taken too far for too long. In a study by the American Management Association, two-thirds of the corporations that reported slimming down their head count one year followed up with the same process the next year. Such repeated downsizings can lead to crippling concessions to competitors and irreversible damage to the organization, especially since the remaining workers are likely to suffer from what organizational behaviorists call "survivor syndrome": stress, frustration, anger, and fear do not make for optimum performance. "Just when you need employees to take risks to turn the organization around, they take to the trenches," says David Noer, an employment consultant in Greensboro, North Carolina. "You end up with a double loss."[11]

The tendency to prolong a Slim Down by executing it in slow motion is natural and human. Leaders often want to delay taking action, recognizing that it will be painful to people in the organization. However, in their desire to avoid pain, they can actually cause even more harm by drawing out the process.

In the pilot phase of a new research project, the Center for Creative Leadership found that "respondents whose organizations had experienced significant employee reductions within the last two years, when compared to respondents whose organizations had not experienced downsizing, [were] less secure in their jobs (67% versus 88%), less confident in their leaders (75% versus 85%), less likely to believe what their leaders told them (76% versus 87%), less likely to trust their leaders (75% versus 87%), and less hopeful about the future of the organization (86% versus 93%)."[12] It seems logical that people in organizations engaged in a prolonged Slim Down feel even less hope and even more skepticism.

---

The emotional repercussions of a Slim Down can never be avoided entirely. However, they can be minimized by slimming down quickly.

---

*You Cannot Involve People Enough.* When implementing any strategy, involving people at all levels is a key to success. Slim Down strategies, however, obviously present dilemmas that are not associated with other strategic states. Decisions about whom to keep and whom to lay off must be made by top management, but many other decisions are best made by others throughout the organization, who have a more intimate knowledge of the workings of the business and where the inefficiencies lie.

The idea that employees at below-senior levels will always be resistant to cuts in either staff or costs is often not borne out by the reality. One executive of a company that involved its employees in advising on cost-cutting efforts reported, "Staff cuts, plant closings, outsourcing and other actions are often greeted positively by the surviving workforce, who start to feel terrible on one level—until they consider the alternative. Their immediate concern becomes, as painful as these moves have been, Are we doing enough to save the enterprise? What else do we need to do?"[13]

When leaders invite more people to participate in the Slim Down process, there is a lot to be said for candor. Using terms like "reengineering" and "restructuring" to cloak a downsizing effort can create a trust gap that inhibits true participation. Pitney Bowes Management Services conducted a survey with some sobering results: Of the largest industrial corporations they surveyed, 83 percent said that they had reengineered their businesses. They also reported that their employees:

- See reengineering as an excuse for layoffs (69%).
- Fear the loss of their own jobs (75%).
- Feel overburdened by work (55%).

As a long-term employee of an aerospace company says, "After promising us there would be no layoffs in our division, management announced last fall that they would be downsizing in sixty days. This created two months of an agonizing environment. I'd say that production went down by 60%, because we spent all our time asking each other, 'What do you think is going to happen?' "[14]

Given the extreme emotions inevitably aroused by this type of situation, leaders of downsizing organizations owe it to people to be as honest and forthcoming as is humanly possible. If you are a senior manager, you may not be able to save everyone's job, but you can at least be candid about the purpose behind your efforts, so that they can keep their dignity and self-respect. Such honesty pays off. When you deal with people compassionately and fairly, and are open and honest with them, they can actually wind up working harder toward the end of their time in the organization than they had at the beginning. As one commentator put it, "The best-performing firms practice two-way communication even when the news is dismal. The best firms ensure that employees know where the company is headed."[15]

*Attend to the Survivors.*   Perhaps the most insidious result of a Slim Down effort involving layoffs is its effect on the morale of those who remain, another key reason for enacting a Slim Down quickly. Even if the change is carried out swiftly and compassionately, however, the people who remain in the organization are likely to experience a great feeling of loss, as well as anxiety and mistrust. Those feelings can affect the organization's ability to move forward.

One company that was about to undergo massive downsizing organized a full-day therapeutic session for its front-line employees. Workers broke into small groups, drew pictures about how they felt, looked at each other's pictures, and wound up laughing about just how terrible things were. Toward the end of the day, the consultants leading the session walked them through the psychologist Elisabeth Kubler-Ross's model of bereavement, to put their feelings into a coherent context. Such an approach to organizational change might sound a little New Age-y, but employees reported that they could resume their jobs with a lot more energy afterwards. Surveys conducted several months later confirmed the improvement in their morale.[16]

---

Perhaps the most effective way of enlisting the long-term commitment of those who have survived a downsizing is, again, to get them more and more involved in the strategy-making process. That will provide them with a deeper understanding of the need for the drastic measures that have been taken and a clearer view of the conditions that precipitated the changes. It can also help them regain a sense of control and belonging, which is often weakened by the layoff process.

---

*The Nissan Example.*    Probably the best example of a successful Slim Down in recent history is what happened at Nissan Motors when Carlos Ghosn was appointed CEO in 1999. At the time, Nissan was on the verge of bankruptcy, having lost money in seven of the eight previous years; its purchasing costs were 15 to 20 percent higher than at Renault, Nissan's part owner. Furthermore, the Japanese system of lifetime employment, coupled with a rigid seniority system that rewarded people for their age and length of service rather than their performance, made many people skeptical that the company could be rescued.

Ghosn's own diagnosis was that "Nissan suffered from a lack of clear profit-orientation, insufficient focus on customers and too much focus on chasing competitors, no culture of working together across functions, borders, or hierarchical lines, lack of urgency, and no shared vision."[17] Just one week after assuming his post, he launched a sweeping set of changes to turn the company around. He created nine cross-functional teams and gave them the responsibility for analyzing the company's manufacturing, purchasing, and engineering functions, to help him decide on what needed to be done to revive the company, including extensive cost-cutting efforts. Such cross-functional teams had never been deployed at Nissan before. Even more radical, the teams included not only senior executives, but also a broad cross-section of employees from different levels of the company, as well as some managers from Renault.

Ghosn then established a merit pay plan that rewarded employees for performance, while also offering stock options for the first time in Nissan's history. Shortly afterward, he closed five factories, eliminating more than 21,000 jobs (14 percent of the global workforce), and canceled contracts with several long-term suppliers who were not offering favorable rates. If such an unprecedented move shocked some of Nissan's Japanese employees, Ghosn's nonstop whistle-tours of the remaining factories and dealerships, where he explained the urgent need for the Slim Down to anyone who came to hear him, made him something of a hero not just within the company but in the country at large. One observer has declared that Ghosn "recognizes the benefits of communication like perhaps no other business leader in the world."[18]

Finally, Ghosn demonstrated in his own behavior the increased accountability he was demanding of others in the organization. When he took over the helm, he pledged that he and the whole executive committee would step down if Nissan failed to show a profit in 2000. It was an impressive demonstration of his own sincerity and commitment, and made what he was asking of others seem much less unreasonable: He was modeling for his employees the kinds of attitudes and behaviors he was demanding of them. Perhaps that was part of the reason that he was not, after all, forced to step down. The company did show a profit in 2000, and by 2001 Nissan earnings were at a record high: $3.8 billion on sales of $47.7 billion.

### Circled Wagons

A business in the Circled Wagons state is faced with extremely difficult times or a crisis so life-threatening that it requires an immediate suspension of whatever other strategies are being pursued. Like pioneers who positioned their wagons in a circle to protect themselves, the business establishes a short-term goal of surviving a potentially deadly attack; it enters the Circled Wagons state.

Business strategies consistent with this state may be as simple as delaying current plans or investments, or as drastic as divesting segments of the business. Short-term crises are often handled by edict management, which may involve cutting budgets across the board or placing restraints on new investments. Other survival techniques include financially restructuring the company, replacing leaders or eliminating management positions altogether, and freezing capital investment. High-level executives, including the chairman, may be called on to "save the company" by making personal appearances or sales calls to preserve key accounts. (They may also be asked to forfeit their bonuses or executive perks, which, apart from cutting costs, can also serve to lessen resentment and improve commitment among those at other levels of the organization who are being asked to make sacrifices.) For example, following the Bhopal disaster and the GAF takeover attempt, Union Carbide (UCC) found itself in a Circled Wagons state. All efforts went toward survival. UCC went into debt and divested its battery, antifreeze, and other consumer products businesses.

As of this writing, the European electrical engineering giant Asea Brown Boveri, a Fort hailed just a few years ago as an example of enlightened management, is in a Circled Wagons state due to a series of hugely costly lawsuits relating to employees' exposure to asbestos in one of its U.S. units. Its shares have fallen by 87 percent; its credit rating has been reduced to the junk category.

Johnson & Johnson after the Tylenol contamination was also in the Circled Wagons state. So, arguably, was Intel with its much-publicized Pentium chip debacle in the 1990s. When it was revealed that there was a flaw in the chip's multidigit arithmetical capability, Intel insisted that it would affect too few calculations to be significant. However, both consumers and Intel's primary customer, IBM, reacted badly to what they perceived as a cavalier attitude on the part of the country's leading chip manufacturer. IBM stopped shipping Pentium computers, and Intel's credibility was severely shaken.[19]

Here are some key strategic principles to follow, should you find yourself in this most difficult of strategic states:

*Take the Bull by the Horns.* This state is obviously not where you want your business to be. If you are there already, however, you do not want to stay there for very long. It is imperative to recognize the threat, to take steps to deal with it, and to move on.

118

Ignoring the crisis will not help. When IBM first came forward with its claims about the unreliability of Intel's Pentium chip, Intel's CEO Andy Grove claimed that "the reaction is unwarranted." When public and press pressure intensified, Intel instituted a policy of replacing the chips only for people who could prove that they used them for complex mathematical calculations. This approach also proved a disaster, at which point Grove said: "To some people, this policy seemed arrogant and uncaring, and we apologize for that." The public relations nightmare ended only when Intel agreed to replace the chip for anyone who requested it.[20]

Although it can be argued that Intel averted a Circled Wagons crisis of life-threatening proportions, it did so by the skin of its teeth.

Circled Wagons conditions, especially in consumer businesses, are often brought on or intensified by bad press and the impression this leaves on consumers (not to mention investors). A strictly rational approach to explaining the situation may not work.

The image problems that Audi experienced after some of its customers complained of "sudden acceleration problems" with certain of its models back in the 1980s are a perfect example. In fact, repeated independent studies cleared Audi of any responsibility, and concluded that the problems had been caused by drivers inadvertently stepping on the accelerator of their cars instead of the brake.[21] By the time the studies were concluded, however, Audi had received so much bad press that it had lost a staggering 85 percent of its U.S. market. Having failed to reassure its customers at the time of the crisis, or taken visible steps to prevent any further "unintended acceleration" incidents, it had to struggle for years to regain its favorable image in America.[22]

119

If your customers think you have a problem, you have a problem—never mind how it looks to you, or even how it appears to objective observers. The more people you have who are in direct contact with customers, and the more input you get from them, the better the chance that you will perceive the problem the way your customers do. That can put you several steps ahead in dealing with it.

*Rally.*   In contrast to the more participatory approach advocated in most of this book, the Circled Wagons state requires a certain degree of command-and-control leadership. The keys to responding to such a crisis are speed and a broad perspective. Although it may be the front-liners who are bringing in the information on which the response will be based, only the leaders at the top have both the power and the broad perspective to make such a major decision.

Top leadership must also communicate, clearly and forcefully, why the solutions they have chosen were necessary, while also offering a vision for the future of the business after it emerges from the Circled Wagons state. Only when people really understand and believe in the necessity for such drastic measures can they become committed to them.

*Don't Cry Wolf.*   When the immediate survival of your business is threatened, a prompt response is imperative. However, too many businesses live for too long in a perpetual state of agitation and anxiety because of a protracted Circled Wagons mentality—usually when a Slim Down has been dragged out and people feel, despite evidence to the contrary, that the company's existence is in danger. The result can be an extreme version of the fear-of-failure mentality that blocks people from responding in a flexible way to cues from the environment.

The Circled Wagons mentality can be inadvertently promoted by leaders who are trying to catalyze major change in their organizations. Instead of inspiring commitment, however, those rallying cries, if repeated too often, will engender fear and skepticism. They can also make the organization less ready to deal with a real crisis when one actually occurs.

Some leaders seem to use the rhetoric of the Circled Wagons state long past its usefulness simply because they enjoy being generals. People will not resist an authoritarian leader during a crisis the way they might at other times. For a leader who thrives on power, who prefers to make decisions alone, the idea that the organization is in a Circled Wagons state can be very seductive. Especially if he or she has led the company through the crisis, there is a strong temptation to keep on commanding and controlling for as long as possible.

## Teaching the Skills of Strategic Thinking

Undoubtedly, the best way to learn how to think like a strategist is through real-life experience. However, it can be difficult to synthesize the lessons of experience on the job. Not only do day-to-day pressures leave little time to step back and think objectively about the big picture, but it is often next to impossible to see the results of an action within a complex system over time. How can you isolate the effects of one particular decision, when so many factors may have contributed to the outcome?

To help people develop their strategic thinking skills, it is useful to augment the lessons of on-the-job experience with more structured activities like training programs and action-learning experiences. The relatively controlled and safe environment in which such learning takes place allows for more experimentation and contemplation, free from the anxiety and pressure of the workplace.

Recognition of this fact has led to an increased focus on strategic thinking in executive development programs and sometimes in workshops for middle managers, but very few organizations have provided people at other levels with that type of structured experience. If more and more people are going to be involved in strategy making, the imbalance will need to be corrected. Like reward and recognition systems, training systems have to reflect and support broader participation, and at the same time maximize its effectiveness for the company as a whole. That can only happen when people at all levels are given the chance to develop the necessary skills.

At Hewlett-Packard, cross-functional product development teams are provided with training on team approaches to creative problem solving. Employees who have not worked on an HP team before are then invited to come up with marketing, design, and operations strategies for transforming a small business, such as a pizza-delivery firm, operating in a highly-competitive environment.

In the next stage, team members put their heads together to define a strategic mission for the project—for example, to reduce cycle time from 50 to 3 days, in order to exceed customer expectations. The mission, kept loosely defined, provides a guideline for the startup phase of the project. Team members are then asked to predict what HP's competitive environment will be like in 10 years' time, what they themselves will be doing, what customers will expect, and what technological developments will have occurred. These visions are related back to the short-term competitive environment in which the team currently operates.

Through this process, team members come to recognize the strategic impact their project might have on HP as a whole.

Next, team members define a series of *"breakthrough" objectives*—the kind of dramatic changes that cannot possibly come about unless new ways of doing things are found. For example, in considering an insurance business customer, one team came up with the goal of cutting approval time for a policy from 20 days to 15 minutes while at the same time reducing costs. Teams identify between 5 and 10 factors that will determine the success of the breakthrough proposition: for example, reducing cycle times for all operations tenfold, developing plants within five miles of each key customer, or making sure that all customers can be serviced within two hours.

They then try to envision what kinds of technological and other changes might be necessary to actually achieve the breakthrough goals. From there, they go on to develop a number of high-level business models, which are used to gain a more complete picture of the overall impact of the breakthrough on the client's business.[23]

The chapter that follows looks at what organizations can do to ensure that front-line strategists have the opportunity to develop that type of strategic skill, and how those skills can be leveraged to create a differential advantage for the company.

## Key Points

- Everyone in the company needs to think strategically about their daily actions: How will they affect the business's ability to compete more effectively over the long term?
- The strategic decisions you make should be guided by the strategic state your business is in.

Essentially, there are four archetypal strategic states, as follows:

1. *Eagle*: Creating a new business, product, market or industry.
   Key principles: Keep the Eagles out of the Fort. Do not declare war on a Fort. Get yourself some risk-takers.
2. *Fort*: Maintaining or improving on the organization's current competitive position.
   Key principles: Clarify the goal. Do it best. Replace thyself.
3. *Slim Down*: Trimming product lines, production facilities, distribution systems, or markets served.
   Key principles: Do it fast; get it done. You cannot involve people enough. Attend to the survivors.
4. *Circled Wagons*: Fighting for the survival of the business.
   Key principles: Take the bull by the horns. Rally. Do not cry wolf.

# 6

# The Front-Line Strategist

Consider the following statistic: In a recent survey on why companies lose customers, the number one reason, cited by 68 percent of respondents, was that they had been "turned away by an attitude of indifference on the part of a company employee." Compare that to 14 percent who left because they were dissatisfied with a product, and 9 percent who were lured away by the competition.[1]

Clearly, the front-line people who deal with customers on a daily basis—salespeople, customer service representatives, secretaries, computer programmers, billing clerks, truck drivers—have a dramatic impact on a company's success. They not only have direct contact with the business's customers and markets; they also see what competitors are doing day in and day out, and how one or more key elements of the organization (like distribution or marketing) are working.

In the past, these front-line strategists often remained an untapped resource. Now, successful companies are increasingly finding ways to make use of their knowledge, skills, and unique access to customers, in order to realize their full potential as a source of differential advantage. They are being encouraged to ask for clarification if they are not sure which type of strategy (Fort, Eagle, Slim Down or Circled Wagons) their company should be pursuing, but also to make their own suggestions on what is appropriate. For example, it was a waitress at the Chicago franchise of the national stir-fry chain Flat Top who suggested to the CEO that the company look into opening a unit in an affluent suburb of Washington, D.C. Now D.C. is the chain's major expansion market.[2]

Essentially, front-line strategists should serve as the eyes and ears of the organization and the mouthpiece for the customer's point of view within it. They should be out there actively gathering information about competitors, customers, and markets on a daily basis, and bringing back intelligence from the field. First, however, they need to be acknowledged, and encouraged to see themselves, as an integral part of the strategy-making process.

You might want to ask yourself: Does your organization actively solicit front-line strategists' ideas on where the company should be headed and which approach they feel is best for their customers? Are they encouraged to help others in the organization understand how strategies are playing out in the eyes of your customers? Are they rewarded for raising a red flag when a strategy or policy is *not* working? But let's begin by looking at the front-line strategist's role as mouthpiece: What does it mean to serve as the voice of the customer within the company? What kinds of challenges does it present?

## The Voice of the Customer

In one form or another, we have all had the frustrating experience of dealing with a customer contact person who admits the justice of our point or complaint but refuses to make an exception on the grounds that "those are the rules." A few years ago, while I was traveling in Europe, I went to the airport in Frankfurt to pick up a pre-booked airline ticket and was told that the airline required me to present the same credit card I had used to purchase it. As it happened, I did not have that card with me. Although I had my passport and a number of other credit cards to prove my identity, the clerk informed me that I would have to purchase a new ticket—at a much higher price—and apply for a refund for the other one.

Patiently at first, and then with increasing indignation, I told her that I traveled with that airline frequently, and I asked her at least to sell me another ticket at the advance-purchase rate. If it was up to her, she said, she would be glad to do it, but the rules did not allow her to. When I suggested that she speak to her manager about it, she just repeated her mantra—those were the rules, she could not do anything about it. I then told her I wanted to speak to the manager myself. She disappeared for a few minutes and, when she returned, told me that he had stepped away; she didn't know where to find him. In the end, rather than stand there arguing and miss my flight, I bought the second ticket, vowing never to fly on that airline again.

Of course, I could have asked to fill out a complaint form, but I did not take the time to do that. And I shouldn't have to. Your customers—most of them—won't either.

---

The people in your organization who deal with the customer every day already know what your customers want. They know what problems are arising and what people like and don't like about your products and the way you do business.

---

Companies often call front-line people "customer service representatives." Too often, however, they see their role as merely representing the company to the customer—explaining, when they can, what the policies are, and if necessary defending them. While this is definitely one part of their job, the other part is to represent the customer to the company. That is the side of the equation that often gets left out.

I would have walked away from that encounter at the airport feeling completely different if the ticketing clerk had said, "You are right, this policy is unfair to our customers. I am going to talk to my manager about it. I cannot promise they will change the policy, but if you give me your card I will get in touch with you and let you know what can be done."

Some companies, of course, encourage their employees to transmit customer concerns. Changes in quality standards at the Hyatt Hotels Corporation, for example, are often the result of feedback transmitted through front-line employees. For example, "a terry upgrade we did was prompted by suggestions from housekeepers and laundry personnel," according to Norm Canfield, vice president of rooms.[3]

Sometimes a customer concern transmitted by a front-line employee might result in an innovative idea for a completely new business. That is exactly how Autodesk, the world's leading provider of PC computer-aided design software, came to create its highly profitable spin-off Buzzsaw.com. This program was born when Anne Bonaparte, a front-line employee in sales, asked customers in the construction business how they used the company's applications in designing buildings and what they would like to see in future products. She was surprised to hear them saying that what they did not need was more computer-aided-design functionality. Instead, they wanted help getting their construction projects completed. One customer told her about a problem he had had when designing a chip-manufacturing facility for Intel. He had sent some architectural drawings as e-mail attachments, but they did not make it through the company's Internet fire wall, and an entire day's work was lost.

After listening to several similar stories, Bonaparte decided that the best thing Autodesk could do for its customers was to provide a better way for the dozens of participants in a construction project to share their drawings electronically and manage their projects from end to end. It seemed obvious from what she had been hearing that a well-designed Internet work space would be a huge success in the marketplace.

The team that launched Buzzsaw.com began by researching exactly how the different participants in construction projects worked. An advisory board of six professionals from different aspects of the construction process was formed to make sure that every aspect of the product would be developed with customers' needs in mind.

Just one year after Buzzsaw.com was officially introduced in 1999, twenty thousand construction projects were already underway through the site. Buzzsaw.com's clients now include large corporations such as DuPont and Walt Disney; leading architecture and engineering firms such as Ellerbe Becket and Skidmore, Owings & Merrill; and many small architectural firms.[4]

### Achieving a Delicate Balance

The front-line strategist is in the tricky position of having to avoid either creating an "us vs. them" impression ("Look, if you don't like it, you can take your business elsewhere") or seeming to side with the customer against the company ("Yes, I know how you feel—it *is* a ridiculous rule, but then so are a lot of the rules around here. It's a crazy place to work, believe me"). Of course, extreme statements like that are rarely heard, but, in exaggerated form, they illustrate the twin poles of the dilemma faced by front-line strategists. The question is: How can they achieve the proper balance? How can they successfully represent the needs of both the business and the customer?

This is not an issue to be addressed by front-line strategists alone. Your organization has to make it possible for them to find the right balance—that is, to serve as the voice of the customer and at the same time represent the company in the most favorable light possible. One way to ensure that they can do so is to make it possible for them to tell customers, honestly, that their concerns will be dealt with. That can involve substantial changes in the way the whole organization operates.

---

Front-line people need the encouragement, the skills, and the authority to represent your customers to the company. At the same time, the company needs to have systems in place to use the information they present.

---

Consider the case of British Airways. When it conducted research into the behavior of its customers, BA was surprised to discover that dissatisfied customers who complained to the airline defected at no higher rates than satisfied customers. Dissatisfied customers who had not aired their grievances, however, defected at a much higher rate. Thus, the company decided to turn their customer relations (CR) department, which had traditionally been a complaints management unit designed to protect the company, into a customer retention force geared toward championing the customer within the company. Instead of being expected to follow formal protocols for handling customer complaints, CR reps at BA are allowed to deal with each case individually—exactly what the woman at the Frankfurt airport could not or would not do. BA has also invested in the technology required to enable its CR reps to access the information customers need without any delay. The CR department conducts monthly internal reviews of employee practices to evaluate and rank strategies for customer retention.

They then place all customer comments in the corporate Caress database. Front-line service people and product development teams have direct access to the database and can decide which problems to address first, based on the frequency with which they turn up in complaints and the likely return on an investment in change. CR reps are also invited to participate as active members of quality improvement and product development teams, so that their knowledge of both the problems themselves and their importance to customers can be leveraged. Since the program has been initiated, customer retention has doubled to about 80 percent.[5]

Companies that expect their front-line people to take initiative and act like strategists may find they have to change their selection systems to ensure that they are hiring people with the right skills to play the new role required of them. Organizations like Disney and Marriott Hotels have overhauled their selection process to do just that. Other companies, like the AES Corporation, the electrical company famous for its employee empowerment, have discovered that hiring for technical ability is less effective than hiring for cultural fit. As Dennis Bakke, AES's chief executive officer, says: "We've made our biggest mistakes in hiring when people have said 'We need someone with such and such expertise' and put cultural fit second. We've been much better off when we've hired people who don't just accept our values but are evangelical about them. I am always amazed at how well some people who have just been hired understand what we are doing and how well they manage to spread the news, so to speak."[6]

*Training* also takes on increased importance when you see your customer service representatives as part of your strategy. At the Ritz-Carlton Hotel, employees receive training in the company's three steps of service—provide a warm greeting, anticipate or comply with guest wishes, and give a fond farewell. Perhaps even more important, according to Vice President Patrick Mene, they are also taught that, "within that process, it is their right to break away from their routine and apply some immediate positive action."

Finally, *compensation* is an important part of the picture. Changing the compensation system to reflect how successfully employees are meeting customer needs sends a clear message about what is important, as savvy companies are increasingly recognizing. The new Wachovia Corporation in Charlotte, North Carolina, for example, created by the merger of the First Union Corporation and Wachovia, recently launched a program to tie employee compensation in their general bank to customer satisfaction, as reflected in a Gallup poll of 60,000 customers, and customer retention, as measured in each separate branch of the bank.[7]

## The Role of the Hunter/Gatherer

Important though it is to have front-line strategists represent customer views inside the organization, such views only reflect the ideas and opinions of people who are already buying from you. It is equally important to know what potential customers in your market are doing and thinking, what trends are emerging, and what competitors are up to.

The information-gathering role, referred to here as hunting/gathering (academics call it external monitoring) has traditionally been ascribed to top management. However, just as people on the front line have a more direct and immediate pipeline to customers, they often have the most relevant and timely information about markets and competitors. What they are less likely to have—a crucial distinction—are the skills to interpret which information is strategically important to the business and the encouragement to gather such information and share it with others.

Thus, front-line people are often confronted with the problem of what sort of information they should be collecting, and how to bring it to the attention of the right people. They may wind up feeling overwhelmed, and stop their hunting/gathering activities altogether, or they may decide that it's not worth bothering, since the information they are delivering is not being used, anyway.

At least initially, therefore, senior management or unit leaders should take responsibility for focusing a team's or individual's information-gathering activities on a specific area. While each business will have to determine for itself what types of information are most likely to be strategically useful, the following are some broadly relevant targets for information-gathering:

- *Who are our primary competitors, and what strategies do they seem to be pursuing in the areas of pricing, advertising, and promotions; new products; and customer service?* People in the marketing function traditionally gather such trend data in a formal way, but salespeople, researchers, and product managers are also likely sources for this kind of information. For example, when the industrial explosives firm Dyno Nobel learned from their sales force that many of their customers were asking for competitor Ensign-Bickford's products, it actually led to a decision to buy Ensign-Bickford.

- *How do competitors' products and services compare to ours?* If you sell products directly to consumers, your own employees may be buyers themselves. Try asking them what products they are buying from your competitors and why. A sales clerk in a retail store who gets five requests in a month for a product you do not sell and refers potential customers to another store three doors down possesses critical strategic information but might not feel motivated or empowered to share it with you.

- *What is happening that is likely to affect our current and potential external suppliers?* Your sourcing function should be on the lookout for such information, but so should others with critical ties to suppliers. A purchasing representative might hear from a supplier that a competitor was offering a lower price to one of your customers. A manufacturing professional might be the first to get wind of a shortage or a price increase on a component you buy from the outside; she becomes a front-line strategist when she recognizes the importance of that information and takes the initiative to raise a red flag.

- *What is happening within government agencies and other regulatory organizations that could affect our business?* In an increasingly global business environment, the impact of government regulation—always a difficult factor strategically—becomes even greater. If you are dealing with multiple governments, particularly ones that are unstable, the insights of your people onsite will be more critical than ever.

- *What changes are occurring in the kinds of technology we use to do business?* In high-tech industries, this question is the essence of strategic positioning. Even in low-tech industries, its importance is increasing. If you are in the grocery business and the supermarket down the street is stealing your customers because they have cash registers that accept charge cards, you need to know that in order to compete effectively.

In addition, several relevant areas outside your own industry and field may need to be watched closely. Specific teams can be designated to keep tabs on economic trends, shifts in demographics among the general population, international political developments, and such cultural trends as increasing diversity in the workforce.

But formal team assignments are only part of the equation. Because of the crucial importance of the individual hunter–gatherer, each front-line employee has to know exactly what kind of information is wanted and needed from him or her. They should also be assured of access to those who are going to interpret and apply the information they bring back. Senior people, meanwhile, need to make periodic evaluations of the relevance of various types of information. They also have to make sure that the channels exist for sharing this information, and that the critical data is incorporated into the business's plans.

### Providing Formal Opportunities for Hunting/Gathering

Sometimes, the best way to find out what is really happening in the world of your customers and markets is to spend some time in it. When Unilever sent a team of young employees to look for new trends and anticipate what the consumer of the future would want, they found that there was a growing consumer desire for better health and well-being. Based on this information, Unilever decided to acquire Slim-Fast, a manufacturer of nutrition and health snack products. Still another result of what Unilever called Project Foresight was the introduction of cleaning and laundry services by the company.[8]

In another case, when Will Raap, CEO of Gardener's Supply Inc., a $26-million mail-order business in Burlington, Vermont, launched a program whereby six employees would spend one day a week talking to customers and developing their new-product ideas, the results were so successful that he broadened the initiative to include every one of the company's 120 employees. Now everyone who works for GSI is encouraged to come up with new product ideas, and, if they look promising, given the resources required to develop them. Says Raap, "For the last holiday catalog, we got 50 ideas from two dozen people. Ten got in, and three to four of them were better than average."[9]

Finally, consider the case of the Weyerhaeuser mill in the small town of Cottage Grove, Oregon. The mill's general manager started a hunting/gathering program that boosted his operation's productivity, product profitability, and morale. Cottage Grove employees, from the general manager to forklift drivers, were sent to spend a week at a time as "employees" of their customers. The shipping manager worked on the receiving dock of a California distribution center, while customer-service reps became sales assistants in Builders' Emporium and Home Depot stores.

Their instructions were to learn, not to sell Weyerhaeuser products. The insights they gained from simply using their eyes and ears allowed them to become more responsive to customer needs. They started to wrap their lumber in plastic and paint the ends according to a coded color scheme. They learned to load the lumber onto railway cars in a way that made it easier to unload at the other end. Buyers soon realized that the field and telephone sales personnel they were talking to not only understood their problems but often anticipated them. More and more they came to feel that Weyerhaeuser was different from all the other mills.[10]

The same approach can be useful with internal customers, too. Some companies send their information technology employees to work on store floors, in route trucks and in purchasing offices to give them insight into users' work processes and spark ideas for improving the efficiency or ease of operation of their systems.

For example, AutoZone Inc., a retail auto parts company, has been sending its corporate employees to work in its stores since its founding 23 years ago. Whereas it used to be a matter of having managers work in the stores on weekends, they now have small, mixed groups of IT employees do quarterly three- to four-day visits. When they return, these IT people tell their bosses what they have observed. "Then we act on those things," says Jon Bascom, vice president of systems, technology, and support. "We made changes to our real-time satellite applications and to customer applications [at the point-of-sale]. We've figured out where a transaction is taking 30 seconds, and if we changed the system we could do it in five seconds."

IT newcomers to merchandising at The Home Depot work with buyers who purchase merchandise for the chain's stores. As Lynda Lockwood, information systems manager, says, "When you go out to the users, you see the pressure they're under. For example, you recognize how little things like improving cursor movement can make their life much better. Once, we found that [our merchandisers] couldn't line up two fields of a report because they were too far apart on the page. They had to use a ruler. We found that moving one column closer to the other would save many, many hours per week when you multiplied it by the number of people who look at that report."[11]

> When front-line workers see their role as the hunters and gatherers of information, creative ideas bubble up through the organization constantly. These people are experts in their respective fields, and their knowledge should be leveraged. It is not merely a matter of making them feel included. They really *are* the best resource you have—as long as you use them.

## The Role of Cross-Functional Teams

As we have seen, more and more people at all levels of the organization are being organized into cross-functional teams in order to break down the stovepipes of hierarchical and functionally driven organizations. Top management teams, by their very nature, have always been cross-functional, but organizations now are creating cross-functional groups at all levels.

At the GE Capital Corporation, sourcing teams made up of people from a variety of functions have responsibility for, among other things, managing the company's supplier relationships and negotiations. The cross-functional product development teams at many companies make it possible to speed the time to market as well as to incorporate a broader spectrum of views and ideas.

However, cross-functional teams made up of front-line strategists rather than senior people may confront particular obstacles and challenges. Interestingly, these do not seem to be attributable to the usual suspect—the organizational structure. When people were asked to react to the statement, "The structure of our company does not allow groups from various functions to interact easily," only 35 percent agreed. Yet 93 percent felt that their organizations needed to improve teamwork and collaboration across functions in order to achieve their strategic goals. Obviously, there are other barriers to true collaboration. It is not enough to establish cross-functional teams; the supporting systems and skills have to be in place to help team members work together well. Essentially, the rules of the game are changing, and team members, especially at lower levels, are just beginning to understand how to succeed in their new roles.

---

To find out more about the barriers team members face, we asked people what interfered with the effectiveness of cross-functional teams they had been part of. These were some of the key barriers they cited:

- *Conflicting organizational goals (79%).* Team members often do not know how to resolve conflicts between the goals of their functions and the goals of the cross-functional team. When different functions are rewarded only for achieving their own internally driven goals, cross-functional conflict is inevitable.
- *Lack of clear direction/priorities (60%).* Team members do not always have a clear sense of what the team is expected to accomplish. Too often, teams are seen as an end in themselves, a way to increase employee involvement. Organizations may focus on ways to get teams to operate effectively or offer training in teamwork, but those well-intentioned efforts are meaningless unless people

*(Continued)*

---

know why a team was convened in the first place. Without clear goals, team initiatives flounder.

- *Competition for resources (72%).* Many cross-functional efforts lack sufficient funding; even more important, team members are not given sufficient time to devote to the project. Becoming a team member should not mean taking on additional work and responsibilities while still performing all the other tasks of the formal job. When it does, the organization is sending a clear message that it does not really value the team's work enough to allocate resources accordingly. Team members will then shortchange their new assignment, particularly if it does not affect their performance evaluation and compensation in their day-to-day jobs.

- *Overlapping responsibilities (70%).* Team members are often confused about their roles: Are they on the team to represent and fight for the views of their own functions, or should they work to find the best solution to an issue regardless of the impact on their specific area? How much authority do they have to make decisions and compromises that affect their units? Middle managers, who may feel threatened by the emerging power of cross-functional teams, sometimes try to defuse their power by insisting that decisions be left up to managers. Robert Hershock, former head of 3M's Occupational Health and Environmental Safety division, recounts such an incident: "There was one member of the Operating Committee who was telling his people on the teams, 'You can go to the meetings, but you report back to me. Do not commit to anything, and report back to me everything that was said.'"

The responses people gave to the survey on cross-functional teams (see pp. 139–140) suggest that team members are often caught in a corporate tug-of-war. They can begin to feel like the mythical pushmi-pullyu from the Dr. Dolittle children's books: a creature with two heads sharing the same body. When demands from the function compete with the goals and responsibilities of the team, progress is impeded. It is no wonder that another animal in the story asks: "How does it make up its mind?"

The problem is that while teams may bring front-line strategists from different functions together, many of the inherent conflicts between those functions have not disappeared. And perhaps they never will. After all, excellence in a specialized area often has a downside for another function. Pursuit of efficiencies and superb quality control in manufacturing operations may mean that less equipment is available for product development testing. A salesperson's desire to respond to special customer needs may be at odds with other priorities in Operations or R&D. Even after reengineering, the 1990s' answer to these problems, demands of one core process can infringe on the ability to maximize the efficiency of another.

## Resolving the Conflicts of Cross-Functional Teams

How, then, can the conflicts that confront cross-functional team members be resolved? Can they successfully serve both the needs of the team and the best interests of their own functions, or will trade-offs always be necessary?

Perhaps what is needed is not an attempt at a blanket solution but an organizational mindset that acknowledges that people will inevitably be faced with conflicting demands, priorities, and resource requirements that need to be balanced effectively on a day-to-day basis. Front-line strategists, like other strategists—and like the organization as a whole—will need to find their own, inclusive solutions to problems that may seem to offer only two choices. In situations in which they need to pursue several different types of strategy concurrently, they will need to make choices about what the priority is. They will need to bring their judgment to bear on competing demands or even conflicting directives from above.

Organizations, meanwhile, will need to actively encourage them to think like strategists, and recognize and reward successful efforts. Only then will their potential contribution to achieving a differential advantage be realized, and only then will front-line strategists be able to fulfill their important role as the magnet that holds the various components of the organization together in the service of its customers.

## Key Points

- Effective front-line strategists serve as the eyes and ears of the organization, and as the mouthpiece for the customer's point of view within it. They are the ones who are closest to the customer, and who most affect how the customer sees the company.
- Through their contact with customers, front-line strategists often get a sense before anyone else of what customers really need and want. They should be allowed the authority to implement strategies that will better satisfy those needs and wants.

The organization can help them be effective in their role as hunter–gatherers by:

- Offering guidance on the kinds of information—about competitors, suppliers, new technologies, and changes in the regulatory environment—they should be on the look-out for.

- Providing both formal and informal opportunities to work closely with customer organizations and find out more about their needs.

Front-line strategists working in cross-functional teams need to be encouraged and helped to find ways to resolve the conflicts between functional and team demands and goals.

# 7 | The Strategy Integrator

An organization's ability to translate strategy into action will largely depend on its strategy integrators—the people who serve as the liaison between different units and functions on the one hand, and corporate leadership and the rest of the organization on the other. Whether they are known as middle managers or given some other, less traditional title, they are the people in the middle, in more ways than one.

If front-line strategists sometimes experience a conflict between their loyalty to customers and their loyalty to the company, strategy integrators face that kind of dilemma on a constant basis. Their loyalty is necessarily divided, because they have to serve such different constituencies. In their dealings with customers, they need to fulfull most of the roles described in the previous chapter. Because they are leaders of their own organizations, they also face many of the same demands as corporate leaders. They have significant responsibility for creating and implementing strategies for their units, which are generally functions like a manufacturing site or an accounting department—or even small business units within a larger organization.

Perhaps their biggest difficulty stems from their positioning between top management and the people reporting to them. They are the ones who have to break the news to people serving on a cross-functional team that their proposal has not been accepted by senior managers—or to try to argue the team's case, if they think it is a good one, to those managers. They have to make sure that people on the front lines understand the company's strategic direction, and its implications for their own actions. They also have to make sure that people at top levels of the organization hear and pay attention to what front-line strategists are telling them about their customers. They have to find ways to serve the interests of both groups, which in the end are the interests of the company. While they also function as strategy makers, the coordination role may be their most critical contribution to the process.

According to Sid Olvet, who retired from DuPont Canada after winning the company's highest award for his services, "To be able to integrate across organizational, business and functional lines, inside and outside the firm, requires a long period of gaining experience and making contacts and friends. In the last couple of decades I noticed that productive results were achieved by ever-regrouping bands of friends, not line organizations. To be an effective integrator also requires freedom, gained by delivering measurable results."[1]

When strategy integrators fail to perform their role effectively, for whatever reason, strategy and action become disconnected. The strategic plan simply sits on the shelf, and even the best strategy is doomed to failure. While business failure is often blamed on lack of vision or bad strategy, it is more likely to be a matter of a good strategy that never got translated into action. As a June 1999 *Fortune* article[2] put it, bad execution, defined as "not getting things done, being indecisive, not delivering on commitments," accounts for 70 percent of business failures.

Strategy integrators, who play such a key part in ensuring that strategies are executed effectively, are therefore crucial to an organization's success. As ambassadors, as facilitators, and as leader-managers, they have three distinct roles to play in the strategy-making process, each of which poses its own set of challenges.

## The Strategy Integrator as Ambassador

The first role of strategic integrators is to represent their units to the leaders of the overall enterprise, and vice versa.

As the leaders of their business units, strategy integrators need to clarify the strategic direction for their people. In addition, they need to ensure that the necessary systems are in place to help people do their work in a way that is consistent with that

---

In their roles as ambassadors, strategy integrators will be expected to:

- Interpret the overall strategic direction set by corporate leadership and ensure that everyone in the unit understands its implications for them.
- Carry vital information and decisions back to senior executives and act as an advocate for strategies created in the unit.
- Coordinate the strategies that have been created in diverse businesses and functions at their own level of the organization.

---

direction. If the unit is pursuing an Eagle strategy by pioneering a new product, entering a new market, or aiming to create a whole new industry, bureaucratic procedures and rigid company rules can hamper the efforts of innovators. (In a more established Fort organization, many different types of processes, from those related to managing cash flow to those governing the way a product is manufactured, have to be systematized to take advantage of efficiencies that have been developed. In an Eagle business, however, some functions may need to be managed differently.)

For example, an accounting department staffed with risk-taking, unconventional people who are drawn to Eagle strategies would probably be undesirable (in addition to being very unlikely). However, accountants within an Eagle organization should understand how this unit and its strategies differ from those of a more established business.

It is the job of strategy integrators to provide the clear strategic focus people need to make their own decisions in line with the unit's strategy. They also need to be constantly on the lookout for signs that current strategies are not working, so they can push for strategic shifts in direction when required.

To perform this role effectively, they must have a clear understanding of the company's overall strategic direction and the reasons behind it, but there is often a huge gap between what middle managers actually know about a company's strategic direction and what top management thinks they know. Therefore, the first hurdle strategy integrators may face is having to explain something they do not understand that well themselves. The obvious solution is to ensure that they *do* understand it—a goal that can best be achieved by making them part of the strategy development process as it unfolds.

This involvement can take many forms. A good place to begin is to give strategy integrators responsibility for the development of formal strategies for their own units. Many organizations now do this, but middle managers should also be part of the process of developing strategies for the organization as a whole. Planning conferences and working sessions that include members of the entire leadership group, rather than the top management team alone, are therefore critical.

Gatherings like this are a great opportunity not only to educate strategy integrators about the current direction, but also to get their thoughts on strategies still under consideration. One commercial bank asked their leadership group to identify possible barriers that could block successful implementation. They then organized the group into teams to find ways to overcome the roadblocks or to suggest revisions to the strategy that would address the issues they had identified.

Another outcome of such brainstorming and problem-solving sessions is that strategy integrators better understand the connections between their units and the organization as a whole. By talking with their colleagues in other functions, they are reminded of the interrelatedness of the various pieces of the business. They leave with a clearer comprehension of how their own units' strategies affect and are affected by the work of other groups.

Understanding is only the first step, however. The role of ambassador also requires expert communication skills and a high degree of diplomacy (needed by ambassadors the world over). Communicating effectively to corporate leadership about the unit's strategies means presenting a logical and compelling case for the proposed approach. Effective communication to people in the unit involves not only a clear and straightforward description of what the overall strategic direction is, but laying out the *why* behind the organization's strategies and the changes they necessitate.

### Communicating with Upper Management

In their dealings with corporate leadership, strategy integrators have a double role to play—and giving each its due weight can sometimes place them in a double bind. First, they represent the needs, views, and strategies of their units. Second, they act as advisers who consider the good of the overall organization, evaluating actions and decisions in light of the total entity.

Neither of these roles—the adviser for the entire organization or the advocate for an individual business—can be overlooked. Many large corporations have been held back by a focus on internal power struggles instead of the challenges of the external environment. Union Carbide is a perfect example. For 25 years, it watched its once-smaller competitors outpace its growth, while UCC's various chemical divisions, battery, and other consumer products groups, gas products businesses, and carbon electrode businesses fought fiercely among themselves for a bigger share of the corporation's resources. Only after the breakup and sell-off of its nonchemical-related businesses did it prosper, along with its more focused competitors, until its recent acquisition by Dow.

However, the importance of the other side of the dynamic should not be forgotten. There is much to be gained from bringing the views of different businesses and functions to the strategy table. After all, Marketing *should* be asking for new products; Manufacturing *should* be looking to optimize production efficiencies. The very diversity of the individual functions' perspectives can provide value, as long as the overall strategic direction provides parameters and focus for the entire organization. For example, if a company's success depends on being the lowest-cost producer, the bulk of R&D activities must focus on reducing the cost of operations and developing products that the company can market, not on basic research.

Although they are sometimes regarded as the bureaucrats of the organization, middle managers have often proved to be more effective at launching and implementing needed change efforts than their superiors. A few years ago, a large telecommunications company that was in the midst of a sweeping change program funded 117 projects. While 80 percent of those proposed by senior management had to be accounted failures, the same percentage of middle managers' projects were successful, increasing the company's profits by $300 million. Sometimes, middle managers' success can be directly traced to their ability to persuade both superiors and others in the organization to provide the resources or help they needed. Their ambassadorial skills can come in particularly handy at times of change.[3]

At other times, strategy integrators may have to take senior executives by the hand and lead them where they need to go. At a large airline, a middle manager realized that most of the senior people had so little knowledge of computers that they were not equipped to make informed strategic decisions about the use of the Internet or e-commerce. To remedy the situation, he set up a program whereby younger employees trained these executives about the Internet—and in exchange, the senior people gave their tutors some exposure to high-level business issues and decisions. In order to avoid too much discomfort, the strategy integrator ensured that no senior person had a tutor from his or her own unit, and that there were several layers of hierarchy between the two members of each pair.[4]

But diplomacy is not always the skill that is called for. Sometimes, senior management needs middle managers to tell them unpalatable truths. When new executives at Hewlett-Packard's Santa Rosa systems division were given the job of turning the ailing division around, they asked eight middle managers to collect employees' and customers' views on how the division was doing. These managers then had the unenviable job of reporting to their superiors that employees thought the current leaders had done a lousy job, and customers were nowhere near satisfied with the products and service they had been getting.

One executive described the feedback as "an icy bucket of water over the head," but it led them to make alterations in their change proposals that ultimately paid off. Middle managers were consulted throughout about how to handle strategic and operational issues. The ultimate result of the process was one of the quickest turnarounds ever seen at HP.[5]

### Communicating with Colleagues and Direct Reports

No matter how participatory the strategy-making process, there are times when somebody has to make a final decision that clarifies and codifies the organization's overall direction—its purpose, the role of the various businesses in the corporate portfolio, what products and services it will offer to whom, and how each business will compete in its markets. That somebody is usually a member of the top management team.

Once the overall strategic direction has been clarified, the role of the strategy integrator is to convince others that the direction that has been chosen is the best among the possible alternatives—the one most clearly supported by the facts, the evidence, and the logic; the one most likely to lead to future success. Even before the current emphasis on empowerment, many people have always wanted to know the *why* behind decisions and changes. Explaining not only *what* but *why* helps to break down the barriers between corporate leadership and everyone else in the organization. Understanding the factors that went into a decision also helps people at all levels to develop their own strategic thinking skills.

---

Inevitably, strategy integrators will sometimes find themselves having to explain and defend organizational strategies that they do not agree with themselves. When that is the case, they might want to be honest about their own objections, while still presenting the rationale behind the decision as convincingly as possible. Their acknowledgment that, within an organization—as within any other type of community—one cannot always expect one's own point of view to carry the day could help others to get behind a strategy they might feel doubtful about.

---

Of course, explaining the reasons behind a strategic decision takes more time than just announcing it, but it is a critical aspect of being the kind of leader people are willing to follow. Former 3M division head Robert Hershock describes the enormous communication challenges involved in a major strategic shift for his division:

I had breakfast meetings and I'd invite about eight or ten different people a couple of times a week and try to explain to them what the issues were and why we were going to change, and how we were going to change. And then I took the Operating Committee with me and we went to each of the factories, and we met with every shift worker. We were there at 11:30 at night and we were there at 5:30 in the morning. We explained what the problems were and why we had to change, and what it meant to them. And even with all that, it's very, very difficult to change an organization.

To be effective, communication of strategies and standards cannot be a one-time event. As one consultant put it, "The corporate vision can't be told once with the hope that it will stick, because for 96 percent of the people it won't. The CEO needs to say it, middle management needs to say it, and the shop floor foreman needs to hammer it home too. . . ."[6]

---

The danger of not communicating enough is not just that people will not truly understand what is expected of them, and will not feel committed enough to give their best; they will also start believing the rumors and half-truths that always rush into any information vacuum: As Mark Twain once said, "A lie can travel halfway around the world while the truth is putting on its shoes."

---

### Gaining Commitment

People will not necessarily feel committed to a strategy just because they have heard all the logical arguments in favor of it. Real commitment entails more than just intellectual agreement; the emotions have to be involved as well.

My company's extensive research, conducted over the past 15 years, indicates that the most effective managers/communicators gain commitment through the use of the following behaviors:

*Inspiring.*   Managers who inspire others develop enthusiasm and commitment to the organization's strategies by linking people's work to both their needs (for example, the need to feel important and useful, or to develop new skills) and their values (loyalty, self-fulfillment, humanitarianism). Inspiring is likely to be most im-

- *Inspiring:* appealing to people's values or emotions to generate enthusiasm for strategies and a true belief that they will create a better future for the company and its employees.
- *Rewarding:* providing tangible rewards such as pay increases or promotions for people who demonstrate the skills, competencies, and values needed for the success of the strategy.
- *Recognizing:* giving praise and showing appreciation for effective performance, significant achievements, and special contributions in support of the strategies.

portant—and most difficult—when the organization is in turmoil, when the work is hard and discouraging, or when the business is pursuing a high-risk strategy, such as market penetration or the introduction of a new product.

Some recent studies suggest that people entering the workforce now want this kind of connection to their ideals more than ever: Seventy-six percent of Americans say that if they were offered two jobs similar in pay and responsibilities, one in a company that supported a good cause and the other in one that did not, they would be likely to choose the company that supports a cause.[7] Perhaps the goal of guaranteed lifetime employment, which no longer seems realistic in today's business climate, has been replaced by the aspiration to work for a company that really makes a difference.

Another crucial aspect of inspiring is leading by example: encouraging people to greater efforts through your own dedication and courage. While the leader should never be viewed by people in the organization as the lone hero, he or she can serve as a very positive and visible demonstration of the behaviors that are required for the strategies' success.

*Rewarding.* Obviously, people are also more likely to be committed to a strategy when they are rewarded for their contributions. Rewards involve tangible benefits. The most common are pay increases, bonuses, more interesting job assignments, and promotions. Other rewards may include increased autonomy, a more flexible work schedule, and access to corporate leadership or important clients.

Rewards can send a powerful psychological message about which behaviors, values, and skills are most needed to help the organization achieve its strategic goals. When you promote a person who prefers to make autocratic decisions, while at the same time espousing a climate of involvement, the message you send is at best contradictory. The management writer Stephen Kerr calls this "the folly of rewarding A, while hoping for B."[8] Such folly occurs frequently, especially when strategic goals are changing. Changes in reward systems often lag far behind shifts in strategies, creating a discontinuity that frustrates management's best efforts to instill new behaviors and values. This, too, can make things tough for strategy integrators—which brings us to the next component of gaining commitment.

*Recognizing.* In some organizations, middle managers have a great deal of power to provide tangible rewards; in others, they have virtually none, or, as we have seen, the organization's reward systems may not support the values and actions that the strategy integrator is trying to promote. How can you gain commitment to strategies if you cannot reward those who demonstrate that commitment?

Even if you do not have much control over rewards like pay and promotions, you can motivate people with recognition—something that is less tangible, but often equally or more compelling. Recognizing involves complimenting people for unusual creativity, initiative, persistence, or skill; giving them credit for their ideas and suggestions; and acknowledging important achievements in a meeting or special event.

At CalPERS, a state agency in Sacramento that manages benefit and retirement programs for California government agencies, a staff recognition program with the theme "You are the Rock" allows anyone in the organization to give recognition gifts such as rock-shaped note pads and rock-theme e-cards to any other employee. A specialized web site also allows employees to give each other day-to-day performance recognition, by sending e-greeting cards.

The second level of the program allows managers to offer their direct reports an afternoon off or a long weekend in recognition of good performance. Finally, once a year, outstanding performers or those who have made special contributions are honored at a special luncheon to which the whole organization is invited.

Employee satisfaction surveys conducted before and after the program was launched showed impressive results. Says Heidi Evans, CalPERS' recognition program coordinator, "In 1999, after introducing the first two recognition levels, our employees' satisfaction rose 19 percent. In 2001, we stayed even with the previous survey. And our turnover rate is between 7 [percent] and 8 percent, whereas the rest of California is between 14 [percent] and 15 percent."[9]

Being an ambassador, then, involves much more than being a messenger of information. It requires not only communicating the organization's strategies in a clear and compelling way but also motivating people at every level to give their all to help those strategies succeed.

It can also mean having to ask people on either side to accept things they find difficult—the failure of a strategy, or, in the case of lower-level team members, senior management's decision to overturn a decision or reject a recommendation. In either case, it is the strategy integrator, the middle manager, who is in the line of fire—and who must use diplomatic skills to gain people's acceptance of bad news.

## Sharing Information and Power

In recent years, as more and more companies adopt a matrix model, the information flow within organizations has changed dramatically. Middle managers were once virtually the only channel for information up and down the organizational chart; now they are sharing this responsibility with others. New processes and structures are creating access to corporate leadership for employees at all levels.

An excellent example of the shift is provided by the 3M unit mentioned earlier. When the Occupational Health and Environmental Safety Division first chartered its new product development teams, it gave each team a senior management sponsor who also sat on the Operating Committee (the top management team of the division).

"They didn't necessarily go to all the team meetings," Robert Hershock recalls, "but the sponsor was a person who could get the team resources, could solve problems. Now, an interesting thing happened when, all of a sudden, teams were connected to the Operating Committee through the bridge of the sponsor. Middle management was getting less and less information. They felt that they were out of the loop. They really started to question what their role was going to be."

Hershock's division addressed this particular problem for middle management through training. ("We really did it backwards," Hershock admits. "We had to go back and train the middle management people and try to bring them into the process.") Middle managers were also brought in as members of the product development teams.

Other companies report similar difficulties with middle managers' reactions to new ways of working. Here are some representative quotes from interviewees:

- "The real squeeze comes at middle management; they wonder, 'What am I going to do, what's my role in all of this?' Middle management has some real concern about how they are going to stay informed, but still allow the groups to perform autonomously."
- "We still see a little bit of resistance at the middle management level. They got to be middle managers by telling people what to do."
- "The struggle we faced and still face was in the upper middle level of the organization; these people really struggle with their loss of power and influence when teams are given a direct pipeline to top leadership."

These quotes highlight a critical shift in the role of ambassadors. In some organizations, new structures and processes are bypassing the middle manager, making a direct connection between senior management and front-line strategists. Middle managers' role in this situation is to serve as a resource and support the organization's cross-functional teams with encouragement, rewards, and expertise. In the section that follows, we'll look at how the strategy integrator can help others in the organization to perform tasks that were previously the province of the middle manager alone. That is another part of the challenge strategic integrators face: Increasingly, they are being asked to prepare people to take over what used to be their role.

## Acting as a Facilitator

In addition to serving as ambassadors, strategy integrators are expected to facilitate the process by which people in the unit formulate strategies. This involves evaluating the numerous options and opportunities that employees identify, and deciding which will be adopted. Empowerment, after all, does not equal blanket permission to pursue any action or strategy; the diverse efforts of the people in the unit have to be monitored and coordinated to ensure that they are aligned with the organization's overall strategic direction.

As facilitators, strategy integrators share much of the work traditionally known as strategic planning: (1) determining long-term objectives and strategies to create a differentiated and sustainable advantage, (2) allocating resources according to such priorities, and (3) determining how to improve coordination, productivity, and effectiveness. The strategy integrator, in essence, sets up the process for judging the merits of various proposals and deciding which will be undertaken and which will not.

For example, a group of managers in the manufacturing function of a U.S. Tobacco division developed a team-based process for strategic planning. They felt that they needed a way to get people in the organization aligned behind a set of common goals and focused on the future. The planning team they assembled involved the heads of the main functions with which manufacturing needed to coordinate. This cross-functional team identified key strategic issues and chartered other teams to act on them. The process was so successful that it eventually spread to every function in the tobacco division, and even to the company's entertainment and international divisions.

As the process emerged, it began to involve people at lower levels. "Directors would ask each other to be on their teams," according to Nick Amadori, the director of employee relations who facilitated the sessions. "Before long, they didn't have enough time to be on all the teams, so they would ask someone two or three levels down to represent their functions."

That is not to suggest that strategy integrators always make the final strategic decisions—though there are times when they will. Because they are close enough to day-to-day operations to know what is going on, yet detached enough from front-line work so that they can see the big picture, they often come up with solutions and ideas that are not obvious to others. At other times, however, they have the equally important responsibility of deciding who will decide. They could do worse than to adopt the philosophy of Danny Shader, chief executive officer of Good Technology. Says Shader, "I'm not this company's product picker, and I'm not its visionary. My job is to put a team together so that the people who are visionaries can do the right stuff."[10]

## Participatory Decision Making

As was mentioned earlier, decision making is not an either-or proposition of group participation vs. command-and-control. Instead, the degree of participation in decision making falls along a continuum. At the far left of this continuum, you will find *group decision making*. Here, the leader has no more influence over the final outcome than any other group member. At the far right of the continuum is *autocratic decision making*. The leader makes the decision alone, without asking for suggestions from others. In between the two extremes is a wide band of *consultative decision making*, in which the leader invites the participation of others to varying degrees while reserving the right to make the final call.

How does the strategic integrator know which approach to use when developing strategies for his or her unit? Research shows that the success of a strategic decision depends on two things: the quality of the decision itself and its acceptance by those who will be affected.

Participation by other people will improve the quality of a decision as long as they have relevant information, ideas, and

---

Despite the benefits of participatory decision making, there are times when an autocratic decision will actually be welcomed. That is most likely to occur when:

- The course of action chosen just happens to be the one that people like.
- Objectives are widely shared, and the decision maker has the expertise and skill to persuade people that the decision is the best way to reach those goals.
- People support the decision maker out of loyalty and admiration, even though they may not agree with the decision.
- There is a crisis, and people recognize the need for decisive leadership.

In the modern organization, however, these conditions are likely to be more the exception than the rule.

---

skills to offer that go beyond what the leader possesses. This is likely to be the case whenever the decision is complex, that is, when the cause of the problem is difficult to pinpoint, the solution is not obvious, and/or any choice requires some trade-offs between potential benefits. Most strategic decisions fall into this category.

Another reason to enlist the participation of others is that, regardless of the quality of a decision, it will not be successful if people who are affected refuse to accept it—and acceptance is likely to be lower if the people affected have had no say. When people have substantial influence over a decision, they tend to identify with it and come to regard it as their own. If they have a chance to express their reservations about the possible consequences of a decision and can ask for specific changes and safeguards, they will be less anxious and less resistant to change. Furthermore, as is pointed out in previous chapters, wider participation creates more opportunities for strategies to evolve and ultimately become part of formal strategic plans.

You should be aware that your perception of how frequently you are involving people at other levels may not match their own views. In fact, a 1999 Watson Wyatt Canada survey indicated that 61 percent of senior managers feel they treat employees as valued business partners, while only 27 percent of employees share that opinion.[11]

Such results seem fairly typical. In the early 1990s, a comprehensive Worker Representation and Participation Survey asked more than 2,500 people, many of them in nonmanagerial or supervisory jobs, how satisfied they were with the amount of influence they had on company decisions. Only 23 percent of nonmanagers and 30 percent of lower-level managers reported that they were "very satisfied." While 63 percent of all respondents reported that they wanted more influence on company decisions, only 6 percent felt that this was "very likely," and 22 percent felt it was "somewhat likely."[12] In their summary of the research findings, professors Richard Freeman and Joel Rogers reported: "The vast majority of employees want more involvement and greater say in company decisions affecting their workplace. They believe increased influence will not only give them greater job satisfaction, but also improve the competitive performance of companies."[13]

Indeed, companies need to establish a process that relies on consultative decision-making.

---

As a facilitator, the strategy integrator has the difficult but indispensable task of determining exactly how to involve people in the process. Do people in your unit understand not only which decisions they are being asked to make, but which ones can be overruled? Do they have the knowledge and skills to improve the quality of the decisions they participate in? Do you know how people feel about the process and their role in it?

Answering those questions requires the ability to juggle the sometimes competing demands of empowerment and coordination, of strategic flexibility and alignment.

---

## Juggling the Management and Leadership Rules

In the final analysis, the effective strategy integrator is probably most like a juggler—one who, after years of experience, can manage to keep any number of balls aloft and spinning. We have already seen how complex the roles of ambassador and facilitator are, what a good sense of balance it takes to satisfy all the different demands they entail. Strategy integrators also have to ensure that their units are performing efficiently and effectively. More than people in any other role, they must be both leaders and managers—perhaps the hardest juggling act of all. And the pressures they face to be leaders rather than managers—according to the conventional wisdom of what those roles entail—may present them with yet another quandary.

The leadership versus management debate has been a hot topic among those who provide advice to organizations. According to the *Zeitgeist* at the time of this writing (the spring of 2003), leadership is in and management is out. Here are two representative quotes from the leadership gurus:

- "The manager has his eye always on the bottom line; the leader has his eye on the horizon."[14]
- "Management is efficiency in climbing the ladder of success; leadership determines whether the ladder is leaning against the right wall. . . . No management success can compensate for failure in leadership."[15]

When you put it that way, being a manager doesn't sound very attractive. But can such a clear distinction really be made? As James Autry, author of *The Servant-Leader*, points out, "It's not as if a manager wakes up in the morning and says, 'Well, I've got to go be a leader today; I've got to enunciate a vision, walk around a bit, assure alignment, empower people and so on.' Nonsense."[16]

There is definitely much to be said for encouraging people at all levels to develop qualities traditionally associated with leadership: focusing on long-term priorities and opportunities, inspiring others, and reinforcing critical organizational values. As necessary as these qualities might be, however, they are not enough to make a business function effectively.

Although it may be out of favor at the moment, management is still a critical factor in an organization's strategic success. Certainly the practices used by effective managers, as identified in recent research, are still necessary to keep a business healthy. These include *clarifying* (communicating a clear understanding of responsibilities, objectives, priorities, deadlines, and performance expectations); *problem solving* (identifying problems, analyzing them in a systematic and timely manner, and acting decisively to implement solutions and resolve crises); and *team building* (encouraging cooperation, teamwork, the constructive resolution of conflict, and identification with the unit).

Even the managerial practice of monitoring, though it is frowned on as a remnant of the old command-and-control mentality, remains a critical part of a leader's job. Those who contend that monitoring—gathering information about work activities and external conditions affecting the work, checking on the progress and quality of the work, evaluating the performance of individuals and the effectiveness of the unit—has no place in today's organizational climate would do well to remember the Joseph Jett debacle at Kidder Peabody & Company. For nearly two years, Jett, Kidder's chief government bond trader, allegedly manipulated its trading and accounting systems to generate millions in false profits. The disaster cost GE, Kidder's parent company, nearly $400 million. An internal analysis issued in August 1994 blamed Jett's supervisors for their lack of oversight and understanding of the trader's activities.

In an even more catastrophic scenario, the unmonitored activities of the rogue trader Nick Leeson, who operated out of Singapore while his senior managers were in London, brought about the collapse of the distinguished, long-established merchant bank Barings in 1994. A writer for *The Economist*, analyzing the disaster, posed the question, "Why did Barings not tumble to Mr Leeson's activities before it was too late?" and answered it in the next sentence: "Nobody was watching him closely."[17] As another commentator put it, "Theoretically Leeson had lots of supervisors; in reality, none exercised any real control over him."[18]

Ironically, empowerment—and especially increased participation in strategy making—actually brings with it the need for increased monitoring on the part of management. People are taking on new roles and responsibilities; they are using new skills and working in new arenas; they are making and implementing decisions that can have a powerful effect on an organization's success. If managers are truly to be transformed from supervisors into coaches, how will they know what amount and kind of coaching is required without monitoring what their people are up to?

Admittedly, the word *monitoring* has some Big Brother-like connotations that are not consistent with the new workplace ethos. However, it does not have to be a rigid control process that robs people of responsibility for the quality of their own work and their own decisions. It may not even entail the physical involvement of managers. Instead, processes need to be developed that are self-regulating and provide feedback to the individual—in other words, Management by Objectives for self-control (as mentioned in Chapter Two, that was the full phrase when the term MBO was first coined). In addition, ways have to be found to monitor in a consultative way, so that everyone has a say in what will be monitored, why, and how.

---

In response to the argument that we need "more leaders and fewer managers," remember that management and leadership are work processes (not kinds of people) and that both are critical to the strategic success of any business. Labeling some people "managers" and others "leaders" is counterproductive—this is another instance in which the best solution is not to choose one alternative and reject the other, but to combine the best features of each.

---

Businesses need more people at all levels engaged in the work of both management and leadership, but juggling the demands of these two activities is particularly critical for people in the role of strategy integrator. They are leaders of their units in their own right. They are also responsible for the effective day-to-day functioning of their units, a role that requires them to perform some of the functions traditionally associated with management.

While a balance between these two perspectives is the ideal, some people will always be more inclined toward the big picture perspective of the leader; others will be more comfortable with the procedures and systems that are so integral to effective management. It is important for people to play to their strengths as well as to develop new abilities, and for those who manage and lead them to recognize and respect that not everyone is going to be the same. Therefore, the real goal is to ensure that the organization has a balanced cadre of people at all levels with strengths in each area. That, too, is the ultimate responsibility of the strategy integrator.

## Key Points

- Strategy integrators—the men and women in the middle—have the difficult task of ensuring that strategies will be translated into effective action. They interpret and explain the company's overall direction to members of their units, and serve as an advocate with senior management for ideas and proposals generated within the unit.

- Ongoing, frank communication is key.
- Use inspiration, rewards, and recognition to gain commitment to the organization's overall objectives.
- Consult others about decisions that will affect them and where they can have valuable input.
- Monitoring is still crucial—but it should be done in a consultative rather than a Big-Brotherish way.

# 8 | The Strategic Leader

There is not much danger that senior executives' role in the process of strategy making will be overlooked. Instead, the danger is that people will focus so exclusively on the lone leader of popular imagination that they will ignore the role of the leaders at all levels who, cumulatively, can have more impact on the organization's actual strategy.

On the other hand, it would be silly to pretend that top management is not of crucial importance in the strategy-making process. To write a book about strategy without analyzing the role of senior managers would be to deny the reality of what goes on in organizations. The fact is, even very skilled and dedicated leaders at other levels cannot fulfill all the functions performed by those at the top.

In this chapter, we will look at the central challenges that face senior executives operating in today's environment, some of which seem to arise out of the very fact that so much attention is paid to them. If there is one thing no top manager is going to lack, it is advice from the experts—and an organization's internal directives often reflect that fact.

What, for example, should a leader do differently when she is advised that the focus on organizational structure must be transformed into a focus on processes? That strategic planning is outdated, but communication of strategic intent is now required? That his job is to create stretch targets or a learning organization or a climate of intrapreneurism? While many of those notions, eloquently put forward by management writers, have useful and/or inspirational messages, they are too often swallowed wholesale, rather than being adapted to the needs and circumstances of an individual business.

A senior leader's willingness to try new approaches or adopt new lexicons is often looked at disapprovingly, as a sign of the desire to find a quick fix to complex problems. ("When companies run into trouble, the desire for a quick fix can become overwhelming," according to a May 2002 article in *Fortune*.[1]) But most of the time, what seems to be at work is a genuine desire to do what is best for the organization, and a genuine openness to new ideas and new ways of competing. Despite the media's presentation of them as rigid and arrogant, most business leaders are notable for their curiosity and their ongoing commitment to learning.

It is true, however, that in their desire to move their organizations forward constructively, senior executives may be seduced by approaches that seem to provide a blanket solution to companies' problems. There is no such approach outlined here.

## The Tightrope Walker

If the strategic integrator is akin to a juggler, the strategic leader is more like the tightrope walker, who requires focus, balance, and coordination to get from one end of that high, thin wire to the other. While those qualities can be demonstrated and debated, they cannot be taught in a one-week course or transmitted through case studies. They can be learned only through experience of both the responsibilities and challenges of leadership. (That is yet another reason to distribute strategy-making power more widely; the leaders of tomorrow are, at this moment, learning the lessons and developing the capabilities they will need to help your business succeed in the future.)

In the context of a business organization, the tightrope walker's three crucial qualities take the following forms:

1. *Focus:* clarifying the organization's strategic direction and vision for the future.
2. *Balance:* helping people to resolve conflicts associated with the strategic focus and remain open to change.
3. *Coordination:* ensuring that the diverse functions and strategic initiatives of the organization work in harmony in the service of shared goals.

## Focus

Tightrope walkers keep their eyes on their ultimate destination, not on the inch of wire directly in front of them. At the same time, they have to be constantly aware of their current position, and the need for small adjustments in that position, in order to keep from falling. In a similar way, effective corporate leaders spend a great deal of time looking forward, while still needing to maintain a constant sense of the current strengths and weaknesses of the organization.

The management theorist Stephen C. Harper calls it "bifocal management," stressing the necessity to focus on both the short and long term, on both operational matters and strategic issues. His metaphor for the strategic leader is not the tightrope walker but the golfer, who needs to keep one eye on the ball and the other on the spot on the horizon where the ball comes to rest.[2]

Because top leaders of corporations are increasingly delegating responsibility for developing specific strategies to leaders at other levels, they rely on broader statements of strategic aims—portraits of future success—to provide the needed focus, alignment, and inspiration for their organizations.

For simplicity's sake, let us call the portrait of future success a vision. Your corporate terminology may call it something else. But whatever its name, it should express what the organization needs to be and is capable of becoming. It is not a wish list, not a description of a perfect organization, but a challenging yet realistic picture of the business as it will be when current strategies have been realized.

Using a point in the not-too-distant future, a vision describes what your organization will be doing for a living. It may also describe where you will stand in relation to your competitors, how your customers, suppliers, and associates will view you, and what you will stand *for*.

The primary purpose of such a vision is to focus the current efforts of the organization in a way that is catalyzing but not constraining. Like strategy, a vision is not cast in stone. David A. Simon, deputy chairman at British Petroleum, describes the role of the company's statement of purpose this way: "It is not self-explanatory but is written in a way to promote conversation. . . . Its power lies in the outcome of those conversations and translations."[3]

James O'Toole and Warren Bennis see the effective corporate vision as a tool of empowerment:

> What has not been fully appreciated about "the vision thing" is that the purpose of a clearly communicated vision is to give meaning and alignment to the organization and, thus, to enhance the ability of all employees to make decisions and create change. The

new leader does not make all decisions herself; rather, she removes the obstacles that prevent her followers from making effective decisions *them*selves.[4]

## What's Wrong with This Vision?

A vision that truly serves as a portrait of the future can be invaluable in focusing people's work and inspiring them to align their behavior with company strategy. Too often, however, efforts to create such a vision produce no more than a handsome plaque on the wall. John Rock, a manager at GM, said what many have thought about the irrelevance of such vision statements: "A bunch of guys take off their ties and coats, go into a motel room for three days, and put a bunch of . . . words on a piece of paper—and then go back to business as usual."[5]

---

When a vision fails to serve the purpose for which it was intended, there might be several possible reasons for this disconnect:

- It is crafted by people at the top of the organization, without sufficient input from others.
- It does not take the current reality of the organization into account.
- It is unconnected to action.
- It does not capture the true purpose and values of the organization.

Each of these scenarios creates a no-win situation, not just for senior executives but for everyone in the organization.

---

## Vision without Inclusion

When a vision is created at senior levels without sufficient input from people at other levels, even the best communication effort will rarely result in true commitment. If even middle managers feel removed from the process and the reasoning behind it, how will a front-line customer service rep feel? If he has been excluded from the process and has little understanding of the reasons behind the vision, it is highly unlikely that he will use the vision to drive his daily behavior and decisions.

Advice about the need for visionary leadership, like advice about strategy, is too often put in an individual context, implying that a lone leader comes up with a vision and inspires others to follow it. Here are some representative viewpoints:

- "To be a good leader you have to have a clear vision of what you want to get done, and keep focused on that vision."[6]
- "Certainly a transforming leader—that is, a leader who is going to transform our reality—is one who has a vision, some notion of where he or she wants to go. . . . When vision is communicated to other people, it motivates them."[7]

Certainly an organization's leaders need to *help* people develop a shared sense of what the organization stands for and where it is going. However, the most effective leaders do not mandate what the purpose and direction of the business are going to be; they clarify and express a vision that people already have. As Scott McNealy, chairman and chief executive officer of Sun Microsystems, said, "Fundamentally, the CEO's job is to figure out what the vision is, not necessarily create it."[8]

Some people and units in the organization will already be heading in the direction of that vision; others may not be. Strategic leaders put the spotlight on the efforts and perspectives that are most important for future prosperity. Usually, it is not that they envision possibilities no one else has seen, but that they find a powerful way to express a vision that has not been fully articulated or given a definite shape before. This helps people see the possibilities more clearly and focus on those most critical for success.

---

The popular idea of visionary leadership celebrates the idea of individual genius. Clearly, this mythic type of figure could be a cohesive force and a great source of inspiration. On the other hand, maybe you and everyone around you have trouble believing in a vision that is not your own. What people really want their top leaders to do is not so much craft a vision for them as to integrate all the competing visions bubbling throughout the organization. That is actually a much more complex task than coming up with a vision all alone, but it is also much more likely to provide focus and generate enthusiasm and commitment. As one CEO observed, "We have found, in practice, that people are much more effective at pursuing their own ideas than they are at trying to follow someone else's."

Just one warning, however, about asking people for their input: Don't do it unless you really are willing to act on their ideas and suggestions. Joseph Weintraub, a business professor who teaches courses on leadership and HR, says, "What employees object to is, 'You ask me for my opinion and I don't hear from you.'" He warns against what he calls the "roach motel" method of soliciting employee input: "Stuff goes in and it never comes out."[9]

### You Can't Get There from Here

Leaders who are crafting a vision often stumble because they place more emphasis on making that vision inspiring than on making it achievable. Many visions fail what might be called the snicker test. If people in the organization read a vision statement and respond not with heightened commitment but a knowing laugh, it is probably because the vision (which may be very challenging and creative) is so far from the reality of the current business.

When a vision fails the snicker test, the process used to develop it is usually at fault. Conventional wisdom would say that you first develop a picture of what you want to be in the future; you then take stock of where you are, and finally you decide how to get from here to there (your strategies). But it actually makes more sense to reverse the process. An achievable and realistic vision can be crafted only after a detailed analysis of the current environment and competitive position of the business. A vision may describe the future, but it has to be grounded in the realities of today.

The vision statement sets some parameters that help senior managers decide which strategies will be pursued. However, in the same way that tactics often drive the strategy, the strategies themselves can affect the vision. When we work with clients trying to craft a vision and codify strategies, we use an iterative process. Their draft of the vision helps them to identify strategic options. If those strategies are undoable, given the organization's current strengths and market environment, or if they involve more risk than the business is willing to take, the strategy team goes back and revises the vision.

That is not to say that organizations and people cannot achieve the seemingly unachievable. But what many call stretch targets—challenging and specific goals in areas like product development and inventory turns, like 3M's goal to generate 30 percent of revenue from new products—are not a substitute for vision. Instead, they are a measurable way to turn a vision into reality.

### All Vision, No Action

Stretch targets can be used to address another frequent failure of the visioning process: visions that are unconnected to action. As one management writer puts it, "there is no knowledge advantage unless it leads to an action advantage." Or, in the words of former Starbucks International President Howard Behar, "A learning organization is useless unless it's also a doing organization."[10]

Many vision statements are too generic to serve as anything but empty rhetoric; if you took the company name off the statement, it could represent virtually any business in any industry. In order to make the vision flexible enough to accommodate shifts in strategy, it has been expressed in such general terms that it becomes almost meaningless. Here is where the strategy leader has to get up on the tightrope and perform his or her balancing act.

Crafting a vision that is both flexible enough to allow for evolving strategies and specific enough actually to mean something is no easy task, but it is an essential one. Lew Platt, the former CEO of Hewlett-Packard, put it this way: "Senior management's role is not to tell business units what opportunity to take. Instead, our role is to create the environment that encourages business managers to take risks and create new growth opportunities. In other words, vision at HP isn't a straitjacket that constrains our managers, but rather a view of the many opportunities ahead."[11]

A vision that includes specific, measurable targets avoids the pitfall of seeming generic while also providing people with concrete goals. Targets can be used not only as shared objectives for the entire organization, but as the standards against which to monitor progress, measure achievement, identify key areas for improvement, and set performance goals.

Metromedia Restaurant Group (MRG)'s vision is nothing less than to "win every guest, every day, worldwide." They translate this vision into very concrete financial and performance goals. Recently, Michael Kaufman, MRG's president, set a goal of more than doubling revenues over a three-year period, reaching profits of at least $2.8 billion.

MRG tracks its progress toward meeting its goals through a process called the "balanced scorecard," whereby nonfinancial indicators are used to measure how well a corporate strategy meets the company vision. In addition to systematically conducted surveys, every MRG restaurant uses a random selection system that chooses six to eight customers a day to participate in a survey on the quality of their experiences, rated on a scale from 1 to 5. Guests phone in their responses and are given discounts or free food on their next visit. The company's goal is for every restaurant to have at least 60 percent of their respondents rate their experiences at five, or highly satisfied.

According to Rod Downey, senior vice president of business processes, the balanced scorecard helps the training department measure both guest satisfaction and employee satisfaction, which in turn helps general managers to meet their employee retention and sales goals and helps MRG to advance its mission to win guests and become a financial powerhouse.

MRG also backs up its vision statement by rewarding employees at all levels according to the quality of the customer service they provide. Not only are bonuses paid to those working in the individual restaurants according to the satisfaction numbers achieved, but even the bonuses of employees working at headquarters are linked to the overall satisfaction numbers.[12]

## The Vision without a Heart

Finally, many visions fail to inspire commitment because, put simply, they lack heart. They focus narrowly on a financial goal like profitability, which, however crucial it may be, just does not engage people's emotions, or they fail to recognize the basic human desire to make some difference in the world. An effective vision includes words that describe the societal need the organization fills. Said one manager, "It's fine to emphasize what we should shoot for, but we also need to know what we stand for."[13] Or, as Goran Lindahl, an executive vice president at ABB, puts it, "In the end, managers are loyal not to a particular boss or even to a company, but to a set of values they believe in and find satisfying."[14]

Such values are conveyed, first and foremost, through action. How does the company deal with suppliers, with customers, with its own people? Which employees are rewarded, promoted, celebrated? Which teams receive attention and respect? Which words become part of the corporate vocabulary? More than any formal rhetoric, those actions confirm the values of the organization.

---

Values may or may not be expressed in a separate document, but they must be embedded in the organization's culture and strategies. In a value-driven organization, every decision is made in relation to the company's core values.

---

At PolyOne, the safety and health of employees and members of the community in which the plants are located is an issue that is continually taken into account. That kind of integrity is also reflected in how the business is run. Rather than making shareholder concerns about the bottom line a paramount factor in the decisions that get made, CEO Tom Waltermire and his team have consistently chosen to invest in the growth of the business.

Medtronic, a $5.5 billion organization whose major work is designing and manufacturing medical technology products, is another good example of an organization whose values radiate throughout the entire system. President George William notes: "Most organizations have a written mission statement. . . . That's the easy part. The more difficult part is getting everyone to buy into that mission and values. That takes time and effort, and consistency of action, through bad times as well as good. It only takes one reversal of values at the top when conditions are tough to reverse many years of hard work in setting the standard and the climate. For better or for worse, as leaders we are better known for our deeds than for our words."

Medtronic's core values are as follows: Contributing to human welfare, focused growth, unsurpassed quality, fair profit, recognizing the worth of employees, and good citizenship. These values are reflected in their business practices, their strategy decisions, and their attitude toward quality. No product can be released to the market until it has been approved by the Medtronic Executive Committee, with a formal vote following a quality presentation. For example, when the Parallel heart valve it had developed failed to meet Medtronic's quality standards, it cancelled the launch—a decision that cost it $30 million.

The company also fired the president of its European operations for covering up a "promotion fund" for an Italian distributor and reinvested a large patent settlement it received from Siemans, rather than taking it as profit. Today that investment is paying off in research on innovative new therapies. Finally, to keep the company's values and mission alive in the minds of Medtronic's 26,000 employees, every year, six patients and their doctors are invited to Medtronic to tell their personal stories to employees. After each doctor introduces his or her patients, the patients explain how receiving a Medtronic product has changed or saved their lives.[15]

Another company that puts its espoused values into practice is General Semiconductor, a Long Island manufacturer of power management components—transistors, diodes, and rectifiers—for the high-tech industry. When Ronald Ostertag took over as the CEO, he held a brainstorming session at which he and a team of managers got to work defining the company's core principles. One of the values they identified was leadership development, a principle put into practice when the human relations staff developed People Plus, an in-house leadership and problem-solving program that uses the company's mission and values as a starting point for individual growth.

The program involves a conventional 360-degree review of each employee using a comprehensive self-assessment matched with feedback from supervisors, managers, peers, and subordinates chosen by the employee. But it goes further than that. After receiving the feedback, every GS employee from Ostertag down meets privately with an outside psychologist to go over the feedback and figure out how to capitalize on strengths and change problem behaviors. Two years after the program was launched, a survey of the 145-member worldwide senior management group indicated that there was improvement in 36 of the 39 development areas.

Five years after People Plus was developed, Ostertag asked General Semiconductor's human relations people to develop a sister program, the Employee Development and Certification Program. "As I traveled around the company, I was getting some very basic questions from our workers," he recalls. "I really believe that empowering employees is the key to any company's success, but you can't do that unless everyone is working from the same knowledge base." In response, Ostertag set his human relations staff the task of finding out what employees wanted to know about the company. "No question was off-base; we took everyone seriously," says the project's manager. Once he had the questions in hand, he then assembled a group of "subject matter experts" to answer them. What HR eventually produced was a 135-page standard three-ring binder of information that includes everything from a list of the company's board of directors and history to a description of products, customers, and competitors to basic financials.

Ostertag credits the attention to staff interaction and cooperation with helping the company to nearly double revenues since 1996 and achieve greater market share.[16] At a time when America is reeling from the revelations of misconduct by corporate leaders and the total lack of moral values within some of its biggest companies, it is helpful to remember that there are not only ethical companies out there; their integrity about values contributes significantly to their success.

### Words and Deeds

Like vision statements, statements of values have to be backed up with deeds before employees will respect them. A former employee of a large bank was blunt in his scorn for the company's oft-repeated credo of "respect for the individual": "It was seen as a pious lie, given their ruthlessness toward people both within and outside the organization."

In fact, even more than vision statements, value statements are likely to arouse anger and disgust if people do not see them acted on. They are not only seen as disconnected from reality and too general to be acted on, they provoke bitterness by the very lip service they pay to high ideals and moral teachings. If disparities between stated strategies and actions make people feel cynical, disparities between stated values, with their heightened emotional connotations, and actions will make them even more so. Better not to make such statements at all than to have them seen as hypocritical window dressing. On the other hand, value statements that are recognized by employees as expressing the genuine beliefs and culture of the organization—in other words, value statements reflected in the actions of the company, as Medtronic's and General Semiconductor's are—can be a key aspect of inspiring people and gaining their commitment.

## Balance

Ironically, a successfully formulated vision—one that clarifies the business's strategic focus—can itself lead to problems. Ensuring that the focus they have struggled to achieve does not become a liability to the company is one of the balancing acts strategic leaders must become adept at. Others involve balancing decisiveness and broader empowerment, and balancing change and continuity. In each case, the most effective leaders aim for an inclusive choice rather than an either-or decision.

Crucial though it is to organizational success, strategic focus can give rise to myopia and inflexibility if it makes people concentrate exclusively on specific goals and strategies. Any unilateral pursuit of a strategy, no matter how good it seems, can result in an imbalance that damages the company's chances for success. Promising new opportunities get missed, and promising new approaches never get tried. In order to ensure that their businesses remain supple and competitive, leaders need to remain constantly vigilant.

For example, a successful startup Eagle business is usually staffed by people who can live with ambiguity and thrive on innovation and risk. In the real world, however, those qualities have to be balanced with some attention to consistency and standardization. An organization whose formal strategy calls for product innovation, rapid growth, and high risk will still need to codify what it learns by moving toward greater efficiencies, financial controls, and incremental improvements in its existing processes.

Consider the experience of Tandem Computers. In the beginning, it achieved enormous success by exploiting a previously underserved need: fault-tolerant computers. Sales increased to $1 billion in its first decade. The company grew to 5,000 employees but still had no cost accounting system. When competition entered its market and profit margins became important, managers found they had no way to collect data on the profitability of individual products. While innovation was still the key to their success, they began to recognize that they also needed routines, efficiencies, and systematic procedures to support their growth.

Large, well-established businesses, on the other hand, face the opposite danger. People can too soon forget *why* they are doing what they are doing, or they may become blind to market trends, relying instead on what worked in the past. Leaders of Forts have to find ways to balance flexibility with control, and maintain innovative ways of thinking without sacrificing the competitive advantage they have achieved through technological efficiencies and systematized procedures.

Companies that are pursuing a strategy of rationalization, or slimming down, place their top leaders in the position of having to balance conflicting imperatives. Rationalizations must be enacted with both speed and deliberation, while maintaining respect and compassion for the people involved. James Autry, author of *The Servant-Leader*, describes this particular balancing act as follows: "The leader must . . . care for people and fire people, sometimes the same people."[17]

An effective slim-down leader needs the ability and courage to bite the bullet, to streamline and cut back operations, though the cutbacks will be painful. Leaders in this situation have to rely on rational and logical criteria and are less likely to base strategic decisions on the needs and feelings of others. Even apart from the moral and humanitarian issues involved, the feelings of the people who remain are of strategic importance, as a company full of demoralized, anxious, and mistrustful employees will not perform well. Choosing the right kind of management team is therefore critical. Apart from decisive leaders, you will also need people with the skills and sensitivity to help employees deal with the inevitable emotional repercussions of the slim-down situation.

In fact, finding the right balance among the members of the top management team can be crucial in more than just slim-down situations. Studies have shown that the skills of the full management team are a much better predictor of organizational success than the skills of the CEO alone. The most effective top team possible is one that encompasses diverse skills and talents, different points of view, and various areas of expertise. It can even be useful to have different types of temperament represented. If you are a perpetual optimist, someone who always sees the glass as half full, you may want a pessimist on board, just to make sure that the potential downside of plans and proposals will not be overlooked.

Whatever their individual strengths and weaknesses, the members of the top team need to share some fundamental capabilities for such a "leadership constellation" to be successful. These include the capacity and willingness to grow and change, the flexibility to allow strategies to emerge, knowledge of their own strengths and weaknesses, and a tolerance for those with outlooks and management styles different from their own.

## Balancing Decisiveness and Participation

The best leaders I know, including Bob Silver at UBS and Tom Waltermire at PolyOne, are undeniably decisive. They are clear about where they stand, and they are unafraid to take action, even when the data they have is less than conclusive. (As Lawrence Weinbach, the chairman, president, and chief executive officer of the Unisys Corporation, says, "If we want to be leaders, we're going to have to make decisions with maybe 75 percent of the facts [we'd like to have]. If you wait for 95 percent you are going to be a follower."[18])

These leaders see themselves as catalysts for change; they take controversial stances that challenge the status quo of their organizations. They are also aware that a vision and the strategies needed to achieve it are not going to spring fully formed into their minds, and they understand that gaining the commitment of the people they work with is of paramount importance.

Wider participation in strategy making means that, more than ever, senior managers must find a delicate balance between being appropriately decisive and encouraging others to make their own decisions. As one executive asked, "How do we change culture from command-and-control to teams? Can you command people to be participative?"

Interestingly, some leaders report doing just that. The 3M executive who pioneered one of the first uses of cross-functional teams admitted, "I felt that team leaders ought to be self-selected. But they couldn't self-select because no one really knew what a cross-functional team was, and they didn't volunteer. So we had to bend a few arms to get team leaders in the beginning."

Even when the transition from a traditional hierarchical organization to a team-based one is successful, there is a balancing act to be performed. David Kirjassoff, former director of organizational performance at National Semiconductor, remembers:

"We had a problem of what I'd call *teamamania*. Actually, in talking to other companies, this tends to be a common problem. But once you start getting teams going, they tend to naturally form and go at a faster rate than they are actually able to be sponsored and guided . . . . There is a tendency to use teams as a kind of first resort, and not to think through when a team is really necessary. Sometimes what you need is a pretty smart individual to go and figure something out."

One way that effective leaders achieve a balance between participation and decisiveness is by clarifying which process is appropriate for which type of decision. Which decisions are best made by teams? Which decisions require consensus? When should a leader get input but reserve the right to make the final call? At what level of the organization will certain decisions be made? When can they be overruled? In every organization, there is an identifiable process for making decisions. In many, however, that process is not made visible and explicit.

The nature of the business and the strategic state it is in also have to be taken into account in deciding how decisions get made. As noted earlier, strategic states may vary widely across the organization: You may be deemphasizing or slimming down one part of the corporate portfolio while simultaneously building new products and adding staff in another. The important thing is to make sure that the strategic direction is clear within each business unit, and that you do not try to run them all the same way. Finally, whatever the degree of delegation that seems called for, it is the people in the units who tend to be the best judges of what systems, processes, and strategies are most likely to spell success in their markets.

For a leader, knowing when to step in and when to back off also requires in-depth knowledge of the actual work being done in the business. New senior managers who are brought in from outside companies or different industries bring new perspectives that can provide the jump-start for major change. The downside, however, is that they may lack an understanding of what people in the organization actually do and how they do it.

For example, when John Sculley moved from Pepsi to Apple, he brought much-needed marketing savvy to a company that had traditionally been technology-driven. But his unfamiliarity with the high-tech nature of the business led him to make promises that the technology could not fulfill (as with the Newton message pad). He also neglected to focus Apple on improving its manufacturing efficiencies, so that it wound up having to play catch-up with its competitors in terms of its cost position. As Sculley demonstrated, it is often difficult for leaders who are new to their industries to recognize when to intervene in the decision-making process and when not to. Again, what is needed is to have people on the top management team with the diverse expertise to advise them on such issues—and CEO's who are willing to listen to others' input.

## Balancing Change and Consistency

The senior manager's final balancing act involves helping the organization to change direction when required, while at the same time ensuring that it nurtures its key strengths and the aspects of its existing culture that make for competitive advantage.

The management theorist Kurt Lewin, who devised one of the earliest conceptual models of organizational change, posited a three-step process: First, he said, the organization is unfrozen from its current state. Then, during the transition phase, the change occurs. Finally, the organization is refrozen in its new, transformed state.[19] However, in today's world, with change one of the few constants you can count on, there is never a frozen state (actually, Lewin himself recognized the fluid and dynamic nature of organizations), and not many businesses can afford the luxury of such a methodical process. Instead of transitioning from ice cube to water and back to ice, the best we can hope for is a kind of continual slush.

The conventional wisdom is that, because change is occurring more rapidly than ever before, leaders must ensure that their organizations change constantly to meet the evolving needs of the market. However, the insistence on the continuous nature of change, and the chorus of cries for transformational leadership, should not blind people to the need for internal continuity.

While it is true that organizations need to develop the ability to change and react more quickly and nimbly, they also need to recognize the value of past lessons learned, and to maintain the systems that keep the organization operating smoothly. Otherwise, chaos can result. Therefore, strategic leaders have to know not only what needs to be changed, and when, but what does *not* need to be changed.

That knowledge comes from really understanding and appreciating the business's core strengths as well as its weaknesses.

Strangely enough, acknowledging and building on strengths is often the hardest part of the task. In strategic planning sessions with approximately 150 organizations over the past 20 years, it is our practice to ask the strategy team to list their organization's strengths and weaknesses. Invariably, the list of weaknesses is considerably longer than the list of strengths. The healthy side of people's propensity to focus on weaknesses is that it supports continual improvement, but minimizing the importance of your organization's strengths can be dangerous, too. Strategic leaders need to remain aware not only of causes for worry, but also of the areas in which their business is equal to or better than the competition's.

Even when your analysis of internal strengths and weaknesses and of the conditions in the external environment leads to the conclusion that major change really is necessary, it is important to be very clear about what you want to hold onto. What are the existing strengths you are going to use to meet different threats or achieve different ends from before? What values do you really want to retain, no matter what other changes take place? A sense of continuity and of a stable identity in the midst of change can be key to the success of the change effort.

### Acting as the Catalyst

When a major shift is required, top management needs to mobilize the organization in its change efforts while still retaining as much continuity as possible. Strategic leaders at other levels can do an excellent job of adapting strategies and prompting new ones to emerge, but it is usually senior people who serve as the catalyst for wholesale change. This is one of the few situations in which the leader-as-hero concept really has some validity: People are much more likely to mobilize behind a charismatic, inspiring individual than a group of managers.

Knowing when the time is right for such a major shift comes from years of experience, finely tuned intuition, careful listening to people both inside and outside the organization, and, to some degree, luck.

---

Once the decision is made to initiate sweeping change, leaders are advised to do the following:

- *Focus on the most critical changes.* People need specific targets for change and improvement—and the fewer the targets, the more likely they are to be achieved. Leaders not only inspire people to reach for new goals, they highlight which goals are most critical for strategic success. Robert D. Kennedy, chief executive officer of Union Carbide, did just that from 1986 to 1993. His relentless focus on cutting the chemical giant back to its core businesses and on reducing costs helped Carbide boost its profitability and left it well-positioned to take advantage of the boom in the industry in 1994.
- *Identify barriers to change.* Changes are often blocked by the organization's existing systems, processes, and culture. Anticipating those barriers and finding ways to minimize or overcome them is key to implementing new strategies and new ways of working. Sometimes, the most serious barriers are individuals who are reluctant to

*(Continued)*

---

change, whether these are legacy employees, people wedded to a particular way of doing things, or simply individuals who are by nature suspicious of change. Speaking of his efforts to create a teamwork culture, one CEO said, "If you find someone who really cannot, no matter how capable he is, cannot by nature, develop into having team spirit, you'd better get him out."

- *Communicate clearly and consistently about the changes that are required.* Strategic change requires consistent and ongoing two-way communication about the new vision, and frequent reinforcement of the business's fundamental purpose and critical values. Leaders who keep in touch with employees through meetings, broadcasts, forums, newsletters, e-mail—who keep the vision alive in people's minds and at the same time invite their input— have a much better chance of seeing that vision realized.

Former General Motors CEO Roger Smith recognized the importance of communicating strategy effectively only in hindsight, and regretted his failure to do so: "I sure wish I'd done a better job of communicating with GM people. . . . Then they would have known why I was tearing the place up, taking out whole divisions, changing our whole production structures. . . . I never got all this across. There we were, charging up the hill right on schedule, and I looked behind me and saw that many people were still at the bottom, trying to decide whether to come along."[20]

How to balance change with consistency, focus with flexibility, and decisiveness with participation: Those are some of the key dilemmas strategic leaders face on their tightrope walk. Are there any easy, surefire ways to resolve them? Of course not. But the best strategic leaders, you can be sure, do not try to do it alone. They marshal the strengths, the knowledge, and the skills of people throughout the organization to increase their chances of strategic success.

## Coordination

Increasingly, leaders of organizations are recognizing the need for coordination among the various units, functions, and businesses in their purviews, to get them working more closely together in the service of the customer.

Strategic leaders make this kind of coordination possible by ensuring that the systems, processes, and culture are in place to allow it to happen. Often, such coordination takes the form of information sharing, allowing key lessons from one part of the organization to be transferred to others. General Electric has done a good job of this kind of coordination through its efforts to disseminate Best Practices throughout its many businesses. British Petroleum (BP) has also found solid ways to coordinate its efforts. In order to disseminate best practices throughout the company, BP has a program called "Peer Assists." Any BP manager with a problem can request the loan of an expert from any other BP division. Not only is this a great way to solve problems faster, it expands people's knowledge of other businesses and the network of their peers within them.[21]

Other organizations are experimenting with giving leaders at all levels experience in various businesses and functions. At AES, job rotation is the norm. People move from job to job and from plant to plant, to learn as many different aspects of the business as possible. Says CEO Dennis Bakke, "Of the original 24 people hired at the Thames plant when it opened in 1988, today two are vice presidents and group managers, eight are plant managers, and seven are team leaders And they're all generalists. They know most aspects of our operation inside and out."[22]

In addition to setting up systems that encourage cooperation across the organization, senior managers themselves often need to share resources as well as information with other members of the management group. By doing so, they become what may be the ultimate cross-functional team.

One organization that focused on helping top team members coordinate their work more effectively was the Tennessee Valley Authority (TVA). In 1994 the TVA organized its top 40 executives into what it called the "business council." "The primary goal," explained Sylvia Caldwell, the Strategic Planning Manager at that time, "was for them to understand every piece of TVA's business, to jointly formulate an overall strategy for where TVA was going, and then for all of them to work toward that strategy. The real goal was for them to be making their daily operating decisions based on this question: 'Does it directly relate to that long-range strategy, and how can we do what's in the best interests of TVA overall?'"

TVA also involved a wide array of key people in strategy development teams that conducted competitive analyses of the energy industry and TVA's position in it. Planning teams then used those analyses to decide how TVA could take advantage of new market opportunities. This broad, cross-business participation in planning was spearheaded by the business council and the executive committee.

Reengineering, which focuses not on the functions of the business but on the core processes required to serve customers, is another approach to the coordination challenge. (A core business process is a flow of activities that leads to a product or service for an external customer.) The idea is to shift the view of the organization from a vertical one—with components such as manufacturing, research, and marketing—to a horizontal one—with processes like customer service and logistics and commercialization of technology (see Figure 8.1).

The main contribution of the reengineering approach is that it encourages an organization to see itself from the customer's point of view, and to focus on those elements that are of most value to customers. This is not a new concept; management experts from Frederick Taylor to Mary Parker Follett to Len Sayles advocated cross-functional coordination long ago. Until recently, however, large corporations in particular ignored this idea.

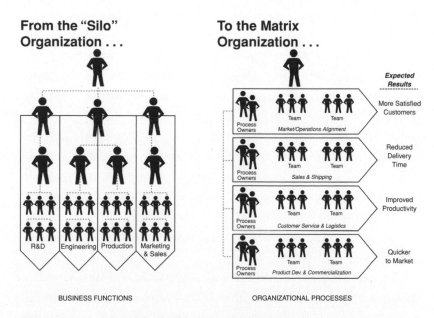

**Figure 8.1**   The Results-Driven Organization
*Source:* McKinsey & Co. © 1992 Time Inc. All rights reserved. (Adapted from Tony Mikolajczyk for *Fortune.*)

In spite of the benefits of the reengineering approach, it will not solve the problem of how to coordinate between functions and units. Core processes themselves, after they have been identified and charted, can become as fixed and separate as functions once were. Look at that graphic again. The boundaries around the core processes are just as distinct as the lines delineating the functions. In fact, after companies have made the considerable shifts and restructurings that let them focus on core processes, they may very well find themselves asking, How can we get the core processes to work together more effectively in the service of the customer?

The truth is, there is no one right answer to the problem of coordination and cooperation between people who do different things in different places, and there never will be. It will be an ongoing challenge for strategic leaders to determine when, how, and how much to coordinate. The key to meeting this challenge lies in accurate analysis of the specific situation, coupled with the active day-to day involvement of management in the business. The precise kind and degree of coordination required will depend on how much the customer needs, either directly or indirectly, the skills of people in various units. In other words, instead of looking at coordination as a blanket corporate mandate, or embarking on it for its own sake, senior executives have to spend time figuring out exactly what really needs to be coordinated in their organization. Only when coordination is specifically tailored to the particular situation can it translate into a source of competitive advantage.

In handling the coordination issue, as in facing the other challenges involved in steering an organization, the strategic leader will have to find a balance between change and continuity, between control and allowing strategic decisions to emerge. Ultimately, the challenge is to create a clear focus and sense of purpose while still leaving room for people at all levels to be flexible, creative, and responsive.

## Key Points

- The effective strategic leader contributes to the strategy-making process by providing focus, balance, and coordination.

*Focus*: Craft an achievable, compelling vision:

- Make sure it reflects and incorporates the input of people at all levels of the organization.
- Make sure it is specific to the business. (A generic vision is just empty rhetoric.)
- Back it up with action.
- Appeal to the values and emotions of employees.

*Balance*: Build on internal strengths to provide consistency in the midst of change.

When managing change:

- Focus on the most critical changes.
- Identify barriers to change, and launch efforts to overcome them.
- Communicate clearly and consistently about why the changes are required.

*Coordination*: Tailor coordination efforts to the specific situation and the specific needs of the customer.

# 9
# The Strategic Organization

*Try again. Fail again. Fail better.*
—Samuel Beckett

We have looked at the role of each type of strategy maker within the organization. In this final chapter, we look at the role of the organization as a whole. Is it possible to define what makes an *organization* an effective strategy maker? Can we isolate the traits that give it the ability to adapt strategically to its markets and its environment without losing its core identity?

Some of the characteristics that make an organization an effective strategy maker have been referred to earlier, when we talked about learning organizations, about learning to live with uncertainty (functional chaos), and about creating a culture that genuinely empowers people and fosters entrepreneurship, improvisation, and tolerance for mistakes. What they all have in common is a positive, proactive relationship to change. In the end, it is that relationship to change—and the very concept of strategy is necessarily about change, about moving from Point A to Point B, or even Point C, rather than standing still—that is key to successful strategy making in today's business climate.

The Greek god Proteus could alter his shape at will to elude his pursuers. When he chose, he could transform himself into a tree, a pillar of fire, or a wild boar, a gift he used strategically to further his own ends. Modern organizations need to become "protean" in the same way in order to respond to competitive threats or to pursue new opportunities, but what exactly does this entail?

As shown in Figure 9.1, there are three key elements that work together in a protean organization to create value for customers and sustainable competitive results.

## Organizational Agility

Achieving organizational agility involves forging a third way between deliberate and evolutionary planning. It means creating a continuous, dynamic process of strategy making that takes into

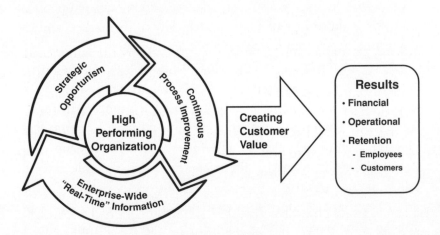

*Figure 9.1*   The Protean Organization

consideration both strategic fit and emergent opportunities, and arrives at a clear vision that provides a focus for the organization while remaining responsive to changing market conditions.

Repeated and widespread discussion needs to take place within the organization to define and refine the value proposition that the company offers its customers. Based on what we know today, what will it take to win? How is that different from yesterday, and how might it be different next year? What feedback is the marketplace giving us, and what opportunities does it suggest? How can we seize those opportunities, and what does the answer to that question imply for our strategy as we go forward?

Acordia, Inc. is an example of a protean company whose organizational agility allowed it to transform itself successfully several times. In the early 1980s, there were numerous changes and discontinuities in the environment in which the company—then Blue Cross/Blue Shield of Indiana—was operating, to the point where the organization's survival seemed threatened. CEO L. Ben Lytle, chairman of the board of directors, decided that the company's structure and approach to doing business had to be changed if it was to remain viable. As things stood, any attempt by some employees to act as entrepreneurs and develop product, process, or market innovations was squashed by the entrenched bureaucracy. Customers' needs were secondary to "the way we do things around here." In response, starting in 1986, Lytle and his company set out on the path to entrepreneurship. They knew the journey would take years, but they also had a firm sense of where they wanted to be.

Their vision gave birth to the nation's largest supplier of insurance products to mid-market customers. The firm's name was changed from Blue Cross/Blue Shield of Indiana to The Associated Group (TAG), and the new company was organized into operating units, batched by industry, geography, demographics, and products. Acordia, Inc., one of the major units created through the reorganization, consisted of a number of small companies (eventually 50 in all) that ranged in size from 42 to 200 employees and never had more than two levels of management. Each company operated independently, assuming profit and loss responsibility for its own organization. The companies' products included life insurance, property and casualty insurance, insurance brokerage, and health insurance.

Each Acordia business was given the mandate to dominate its current market niche while at the same time developing new ones. New venture teams were formed, consisting of people from different functional backgrounds and organized around distinct customer needs according to industry type, geographic area, demographic characteristics, and products. These teams were responsible for coming up with process, product, and market innovations.

A company-wide compensation system was developed that was focused on performance outcomes, to encourage entrepreneurship. A CEO's annual compensation was based on his or her company's financial performance, but also on the results of customer satisfaction surveys, the quality of a company's product and geographic diversification, and surveys of employee satisfaction with the manager's performance, especially as it related to her or his ability to foster and support entrepreneurial actions.

In one typical Acordia company, dedicated to developing, marketing and administering innovative insurance-related products to small businesses, a one-floor facility helped to encourage interactions among employees that led to brainstorming and the free exchange of ideas. In addition, an Employee Advisory Council, its members elected by their peers, was established to find ways to continually improve the company's products.

Acordia's corporate entrepreneurship strategy was a success.

New venture teams put together employees with all the diverse skills needed to innovate, rather than keeping people within their own functions. The horizontal management structure and decentralized decision making practices of the company empowered people to respond rapidly to market opportunities. Innovative internal processes helped to streamline company operations. The firm became more diversified in its products and markets, in that new products were introduced into multiple markets, while new markets with specific customer needs were regularly identified. The commitment to serve new, highly focused markets led to the creation of additional Acordia companies throughout the early 1990s.

Then, in 1995, an analysis of the external environment suggested that healthcare would be delivered, paid for, and administered in substantially different ways in the future, and that rapid consolidation would take place. At that point, TAG decided to change its focus on product and geographic diversification and refocus on core healthcare-insurance product lines.

As a direct result of this decision, all healthcare insurance businesses were transferred from Acordia to TAG. Acordia was then sold to a group of investors and company officers in 1997, creating the largest privately held property/casualty brokerage company in the world. It adopted a growth strategy that entailed the purchase of several smaller, local U.S. brokerage firms with outstanding reputations and a similar business philosophy to Acordia's. It also formed strategic partnerships with companies like Merck–Medco, the country's largest prescription benefits manager. The two firms pooled their resources to develop a private-label prescription program offered exclusively through Acordia, which continues to thrive by offering global reach with local expertise, while remaining committed to developing innovative products and innovative ways of delivering them.[1]

## Continuous Process Improvement

You could say that continuous process improvement—the ongoing quest to improve productivity and quality and to reduce the number of transactions in the company's business operations—is to strategy making what the back office is to the front office. While it is essential to achieving superior performance, it is not sufficient in itself to create the kind of sustainable difference that yields a competitive advantage. As Michael Porter says, "There's a fundamental distinction between strategy and operational effectiveness. Strategy is about making choices, trade-offs; it's about deliberately choosing to be different. Operational effectiveness is about things that you really shouldn't have to make choices on; it's about what's good for everybody and about what every business should be doing."[2]

Rather than being an element of strategy, then, it is an integral part of the successful deployment and execution of any given strategy. It must itself be approached strategically, since the decision about *which* specific processes to focus on *when* is key. Processes that have been carefully selected based on their strategic importance, such as supply-chain management and new product development, need to be scrutinized, taken apart, and put back together more efficiently and effectively in order to improve the protean organization's effectiveness.

The concept of business process improvement can be traced back to the work of pioneering management expert Frederick Taylor, whose initial work in the field inspired a series of approaches such as industrial engineering, operations research, and work-process analysis. The past couple of decades have seen the rise of yet further approaches to business process improvement. They have gone by various names: total quality management (TQM), benchmarking, business process reengineering (BPR), *kaizen*, and lean manufacturing. Total quality management and business process reengineering are sometimes seen as diametrically opposed—TQM emphasizes constant, progressive change, while BPR advocates a clean-slate approach: large-scale changes based on a fundamental rethinking of the business, and involving sweeping process redesign and reengineering. However, in spite of their differences, some management experts regard them as compatible, and argue that, instead of choosing between the two, the more effective way to bring about business process improvement is to use both.

The dilemma inherent in continuous process improvement is that the effort to ensure that processes are repeatable, predictable, and rigorous can result in processes that are rigid and calcified. How can an organization maintain predictable processes while also remaining constantly changing and improving? How can it ensure that it will not become so process-oriented that it starts focusing on processes for their own sake, rather than on adding value for customers? That is what happened at several high-profile organizations. Florida Power & Light, for example, won the coveted Deming Prize—the only American company to do so—and then discovered that the rigorous Deming methodology they had adopted was diverting employees' attention and energies from results and substance to slavishly following procedural protocol.[3] Similarly, the Wallace Company, a Houston pipe and valve distributor, went bankrupt two years after winning the Baldridge Award, in part because it stopped focusing on its customers and focused on its TQM programs instead.[4]

---

In the ideal protean organization, continuous improvement of business processes takes place within an organizational structure that is networked, fluid, and customer oriented. A flexible structure both facilitates the achievement of scale economies and allows for innovative responses to market needs as they arise. An emphasis on the customer and on achieving strategic goals ensures that process will not become the central focus; instead of being seen as an end in itself, it will be seen, rightly, as a means to an end—a way of supporting strategy making as a dynamic learning process.

---

A good example of continuous process improvement specifically geared to supporting strategy is the training program that Ford Motor Company launched at Halewood, a former Ford Escort plant in the United Kingdom, to ensure that the new Baby Jag, which was the linchpin of Ford's strategy for Jaguar, would roll off the assembly line on time and would meet or exceed quality standards.

Once known for intractable production and labor problems, Halewood—whose physical plant also received a major overhaul—was transformed into what one observer called "a shining model of empowerment and teamwork" through extensive training of the 3,000-member workforce and a new, team-based structure.

The process began in November 1998, when a new plant manager was appointed. He selected 14 people, 11 of whom were new to Halewood, to serve on an operations committee. One-on-one interviews with senior and middle managers and focus groups with randomly selected supervisors, engineers, production workers, and office staff were used to identify the issues that the training program needed to address. Almost all employees were invited to participate in workshops conducted by internal volunteers who had been trained for the purpose. Between January 1999 and March 2000, these internal facilitators, who included line supervisors, industrial engineers, and hourly line workers, led 120 experiential workshops that focused on skills like teamwork, leadership, building interpersonal relationships, and thinking outside the box—the same skills that had been taught in the workshops attended by senior managers. Participants acted out a series of typical factory floor scenarios that were interrupted at key junctures and then analyzed. These analyses dramatically highlighted the old beliefs, prejudices, and behaviors that could easily sabotage their primary objective, which was to create a quality product on time and within budget.

An additional benefit of the workshops was that workers who had previously expressed the feeling that they were not being listened to had a chance to talk with managers in an environment that was open and safe. Similarly, the managers came to sympathize more readily with workers' concerns. Participants at all levels began to see how they could achieve necessary improvements.

One of the symbols of the newly empowered workforce is a bright orange cord that weaves its way around the assembly room. Any worker can tug on it to stop the assembly line when a problem crops up, rather than, as in the past, having to call a supervisor who might or might not show up.

Another key part of the program was the "centers of excellence" program adopted by Halewood in January 1999. This called for specified areas of the plant to become standard-bearers of best practices, defined in terms of the types of work practices that would be required to build the new Baby Jag. Every six weeks, an additional four or five areas were added. These initiatives, which Jaguar calls the Halewood Difference, resulted in a 20 percent productivity improvement in less than 18 months, well before the full transition to Jaguar manufacturing.[5] Although Ford is still having problems marketing Jaguars, the manufacturing process itself remains one of the company's big successes in that area.

## Enterprise-Wide Real-Time Information

Thanks to the rapid advances in technology that have revolutionized the way companies do business, all employees in any type of organization can now have instant access to the information they require to make day-to-day decisions, modify existing strategies, and identify emergent ones. Resources can be allocated where and as needed; information of direct value to customers can be accessed in real time, allowing decisions to be made in accordance with customer needs and market opportunities.

Again, this is not a strategy in itself; the strategic aspect lies in designing the information architecture so that it both reflects the way people actually work and directly contributes to adding value for customers. In every case, the question that must be asked is not, How efficient is this system? or How much more information will it make available? but What do customers want that this system will make it possible for us to provide? The belief that pooling information is an end in itself is not only misguided; it can actually be harmful to an organization's success.

Another dilemma presented by the availability of enterprise-wide real-time information is that, surprisingly, sometimes it becomes a tool for *dis*empowerment. Senior managers who have access to all the information required for making decisions may be tempted to go ahead and make them on their own. This problem arises, however, only in organizations that do not have a genuine culture of empowerment. In those that do, real-time information is the ultimate conferrer of power on people at all levels. Those on the front lines who can relate what is in the system to what is going on before their eyes are much better able to see the effects of their actions and make informed decisions.

That kind of empowerment through information transformed the Mitre Corporation, a federally funded research and development center based in Massachusetts and Virginia. Mitre's clients include the Department of Defense, the Internal Revenue Service (IRS), and the Federal Aviation Administration (FAA); its innovative products have ranged from the Airborne Warning and Control System to an intranet for the U.S. intelligence community. The Mitre Information Infrastructure (MII), a web-based knowledge bank that stores information about everything the organization does, has changed Mitre's culture from one of three separate and often competing fiefdoms with their own closely guarded areas of expertise to what its president, Victor A. DeMarines, calls "a culture of sharing."

When DeMarines took office in 1996, he was confronted with a situation in which no one even knew who the in-house experts in a given area were, let alone being able to call on their knowledge. DeMarines realized that the organization would need an information architecture that not only enabled sharing, but actively encouraged it. As Andrea Weiss, a 20-year veteran of the company who became its first CIO in 1997, says, "If you wanted an answer to a question, you had to have a 'people network.' You needed to know someone who knew someone who knew who was expert in what."

DeMarines asked Weiss to help him tackle the problem. There was already a fairly basic TCP/IP-based network at the company, which offered employees access to Mitre's employee directory, administrative policies, and corporate information. Weiss set about enriching this intranet with the information employees would need to do their jobs better. She and her team met not just with managers but with people at all levels of the organization and identified a set of business requirements that led them to design another type of corporate directory—one that went beyond names and numbers to include personal profiles and resumes for each employee, as well as the texts of their professional publications.

Another feature of the new system was a Systems Engineering Process Library that focused on lessons learned: best practices of key software systems used at Mitre. The Risk Assessment and Management Program detailed 10 years' worth of lessons learned from all Mitre projects. Other features of the system included time cards, expense sheets, applications for meeting space, and the company phone directory—all the practical forms and information people needed, made available in a less cumbersome form. "We were looking for hooks to get people into MII," Weiss explains. "And once we've got someone there, they're going to spend some time with it."

Says Harold Sorenson, senior vice president and general manager of Mitre's Center for Air Force C2 Systems, "We're behaving dramatically differently today than we were two years ago." Some of the major differences from the old days of a fiefdom-style organization, according to Sorenson, are that people now talk knowledgably about Mitre projects they've never worked on themselves, and collaborate with people they would once never even have spoken to.

More than 4,000 employees interact with the system daily, and MII's primary web servers record up to 10 million transactions every month. Each of Mitre's business units has programs underway to further leverage MII, and a new MII extranet allows selected customers to access project information as well as technical expertise. For those customers without access to the extranet, internal expertise is still available within moments, since anyone in the company can instantly locate the in-house expert with the answers.

Since its inception, MII has netted an ROI of $54.91 million in reduced operating costs and increased productivity. It also won Mitre an Enterprise Value Award in 1999. The judges called MII "a very robust, rich and widely used set of management tools. . . . The extent of use was remarkable, and given what Mitre is—a knowledge management organization—these tools advance the very core of their being." To put it another way, the system enables everyone at Mitre to translate the company's mission into reality: "Solutions that make a difference." "It's not just a jingle," says Weiss. "It's the way of life for us."[6]

## The High-Performing Strategy Maker

Ultimately, in a business of the type we have been looking at—a protean organization that has achieved organizational agility, practices strategic process improvement on an ongoing basis, and makes strategic use of enterprise-wide real-time information—the organization and the strategy become melded together. The organization's identity *is* its strategic focus, and its focus is what defines it.

How does this concept square with the idea of being protean, of constant change? As we have seen, changing strategies in adaptation to changes in your markets and your environment does not mean changing strategic focus. A focus on meeting customer needs, for example, can encompass a broad variety of strategies as those needs change.

At Dyno Nobel, a global manufacturer of explosives and initiation systems for commercial markets, the focus on customer needs is so well-embedded in the organization that, as Jim Bayliss, vice president of global operations initiation systems, puts it, "it would be hard for anyone working here not to think about that, whatever they were doing." The sales reps in the field, the technical people, and the people who deliver to distributors, are all encouraged to spend a lot of time just talking to the people they serve. They come back with a great deal of useful information about both customers and competitors, which in turn feeds into the company's strategies. Says Bayliss, "Ideas flow in very easily, and get broad visibility. Ideas also come from the shop floor. It's the people who are actually involved in the manufacturing process who know what needs to be improved and how to go about it." It is their knowledge, perhaps, that accounts for The Ensign-Bickford Company (EBCo), a major manufacturer that recently merged with Dyno Nobel, having won the coveted 2002 Shingo Prize for Excellence in Manufacturing (what *Business Week* calls "the Nobel Prize of manufacturing").

In keeping with their focus on providing value to the customer, in the late 1990s, after many years of being organized into functional silos, EBCo reorganized its structure around the value stream, beginning with the supplier right through to the customer. According to Bayliss, then EBCo's vice president of operations,

> That really changed everything. People from all different areas are sitting at desks next to each other now, so cross-functional communication goes on at the coffeepot all through the day, as well as through more formal channels. That's where a lot of the ideas bubble up. And people are free to go to whomever they need to see to discuss their ideas. There are not a lot of filters, there's not a lot of hierarchy. People can go see someone a couple of levels up, without going through their direct superiors. People here are comfortable enough with their own positions not to feel upset when someone bypasses them and goes to the top.

When it changed its organizational structure to allow for greater responsiveness, EBCo also recognized the need for real-time information that would allow everyone in the company to know how well the business processes were working at any given moment. In a sense, the reorganization itself made it possible for enterprise-wide information to flow back and forth, without relying on software per se to accomplish that goal. It is the identification of business processes and metrics that is the real job, not the installation of a system.

At Dyno Nobel, where EBCo's principle of organizing its structure around the value stream is being adopted across the organization, it is the operations people, not the IT people per se, who determine what systems are needed. Essentially, they also design those systems, with IT support. The IT people, however, are full members of the business team, and are fully integrated into the business. They always participate in continuous improvement events, and they serve on many cross-functional teams; their understanding of the business, says Bayliss, is "superb. And their performance reviews are based on feedback from operations people and others, as well as their functional boss."

At the same time that it was redesigning its organizational structure, EBCo also realized that more and more work would be done in teams, which in turn would require greater team-building skills among its employees. It hired a firm of consultants to train selected employees to act as facilitators, and these employees trained others in turn.

The cross-functional teams at Dyno Nobel are responsible for new products, for problem-solving, for continuous process improvement, and for increasing efficiencies. Engineers, manufacturing people, salespeople, and marketing people might all come together on a project. There are also high-performance work teams on the factory floor. Each team has a traditional Star Point system, whereby one team member is assigned responsibility for a specific aspect of the team's performance, and there are designated channels for taking issues to management if they cannot be resolved. In the case of process improvements or projects like decreasing manufacturing time, the goals of the project are posted throughout the workplace, along with information on current performance.

---

The team structure supports creativity more than any-thing else we've experienced, because people have all the resources right there. If they need an engineer, they've got an engineer. If they need someone with marketing savvy, they've got that person. At the same time, the team screens out the kind of silly ideas we sometimes used to get when we had a suggestion program. We don't need that any more. Instead of a few people sorting through a snowstorm of ideas, the teams are responsible for decid-ing which ones are worth spending time on. The real dif-ference is that before, you might come up with an idea but take no responsibility for it. Now you've got the idea and the responsibility for implementing it.

   —Jim Bayliss, VP,
    Global Operations Initiation Systems,
    Dyno Nobel

---

Any technical representative in the field, or anyone on the factory floor, can fill out a form outlining a new idea—for a prod-uct, a service improvement, a process improvement, a solution to a customer problem—and if it seems viable, a cross-functional team will be formed to explore it further. Dyno Nobel's manage-ment not only supports the teams' activities by making sure they have the resources they need—including real-time information that allows everyone in the company to know how things are working at any given time—they have also established regulations to ensure team empowerment. At the former EBCo plants, any idea that cost less than $10,000 to implement required no formal approval from anyone above the team leader. It could just be translated into action immediately. "Before," says Bayliss, "it was the engineers and the scientists who were the creative ones. Now, it's everyone. Everyone around here is coming up with ideas for making the business better."[7]

## Learning to Love Change

Heraclitus, who lived more than 2,500 years ago, said, "Nothing endures but change." Darwin wrote, "It's not the strongest species that survive, nor the most intelligent, but the ones most responsive to change."

At Dyno Nobel and other protean companies, change, in both the environment and the organization itself, is accepted as a given. Rather than being feared and dreaded, it is even welcomed as an opportunity. Because such companies are positioned—by virtue of their agility, real-time information, and culture of continuous learning—to adapt to and take advantage of change, they can embrace it when it comes. They can choose freely among the available alternatives, or come up with new ones that nobody else has thought of before.

That does not mean, however, that they have arrived at a perfect strategic state. In fact, one of the most important lessons every leader needs to absorb is that there can be no such thing. As long as organizations are run by human beings, they will never attain perfection. Businesses are continually lurching toward entropy, and none of them is ever going to get everything exactly right. It is precisely because mistakes will always be made that learning from them is so crucial to success.

But imperfect organizations can still remain healthy, make effective strategic choices, and achieve robust or even spectacular growth, as long as they are agile enough to go on learning from their past experiences, both the positive and the negative ones.

Just as the most effective individuals are those who are capable of learning from their experiences, the most effective organizations are those where there is a continuous, collective process of learning from what has gone before. It is then that the strategic choices presented in this book can be made from a position of strength.

## Key Points

- In a constantly changing environment, organizations themselves need to be able to transform themselves continuously in order to succeed.
- Such ongoing transformation requires:

    *Strategic opportunism*: a strategy-making process that takes into consideration both strategic fit and emergent opportunities.

    *Continuous improvement* of business processes, approached strategically.

    *Enterprise-wide, real-time information*, specifically geared and structured to provide value to customers.

- Continuous transformation does not mean losing strategic focus. Strategies may change, but focus should not.
- In a high-performing organization, the strategy and the organization are melded together. The business's strategic focus becomes its identity.

# Notes

## Preface

1. W.G. Sebald. *Austerlitz*. New York: Random House, 2001.

## Chapter 1  A New Approach to Strategy

1. Kambil Ajit, G. Bruce Friesen, and Arul Sundaram. "Co-Creation: A new source of value." *Outlook* 2 (1999): p. 38.
2. Ian McDonald Wood. "E-Culture: Creating the Networked Organization." *CAI Journal* (February 2001).
3. Gary Hamel and C.K. Pralahad. *Competing for the Future*. Boston: Harvard Business School Press, 1994.
4. Henry Mintzberg, Bruce Ahlstrand, and Joseph Lampel. *Strategy Safari: A Guided Tour through the Wilds of Strategic Management*. New York: The Free Press, 1998: p. 69.
5. Alan G. Robinson and Sam Stern. *Corporate Creativity: How Innovation and Improvement Actually Happen*. San Francisco: Berrett-Koehler Publishers, 1997: p. 8.
6. Susan Greco. "Where Great Ideas Come From." *Inc.* (April 1998): p. 076.
7. Jim Carlton. "Newton's Fate Seen as Lesson for Industry." the *Wall Street Journal Europe* (March 2, 1998).
8. *Business Week* (February 18, 1967): p. 202.

9. Keith H. Hammonds. "Grassroots Leadership—Ford Motor Co." *Fast Company* (April 2000).

10. Orit Gadiesh. "Transforming Corner-Office Strategy into Front-Line Action." *Harvard Business Review* 79 (May 2001): p. 5.

11. Interview with Robert Silver, October 2001.

12. Laird Harrison. "We're All the Boss: Giving workers stock helps a firm only if it also gives them a say in how the place is run." *Time* 159 (April 8, 2002): i14, pY10+.

13. Paul Britton and C. Terrence Walker. "Beyond carrot and stick." *Ivey Business Quarterly* 62 (Winter 1997): n2, p. 50(6).

14. Victoria Griffith. "Emergent Leadership: Bringing Free-Market Risks and Rewards to Command-and-Control Corporations." Fourth Quarter, 1998.

15. "3M Worldwide: Innovation Chronicles." www.3M.com.

## Chapter 2 *Challenges in Strategy Making*

1. Ramona Dzinkowski. "Mission Possible." *CMA Management* (February 2000).

2. William J. Holstein. "Dump the Cookware." *Business* 2.0 (May 1, 2001).

3. Wayne Koberstein. "Merck stays in stride: a strategic update from chairman Ray Gilmartin" (executive profile). *Pharmaceutical Executive* 22 (October 2002): i10 p. 48.

4. Ramona Dzinkowski. "Mission Possible." *CMA Management* (February 2000).

5. Rosbeth Moss Kanter, John Kao, and Fred Wiersama, eds. *Innovation: Breakthrough Ideas at 3M, DuPont, GE, Pfizer, and Rubbermaid.* New York: HarperCollins, 1997: pp. 114–115.

6. Alan G. Robinson and Sam Stern. *Corporate Creativity: How Innovation and Improvement Actually Happen.* San Francisco: Berrett-Koehler Publishers, 1998.

7. Susannah Clark. "Long Distance Calling." *Continental Magazine* (July 2001): pp. 44–47.

8. Jane Lewis. "Charting the evolution of strategic HR." *Personnel Today* (October 8, 2002): p. 20.

9. Kanter et al., *Innovation*, p. 113 ff.

10. Ibid., pp. 70–71.

11. Ibid., p. 50.

12. Robert G. Eccles and Nitin Nohria. *Beyond the Hype: Rediscovering the Essence of Management.* Boston: Harvard Business School Press, 1992.

13. Patrick Oster. "How a New Boss Got ConAgra Cooking Again." *Business Week* (July 25, 1994): p. 73.

14. Shantanu Dutta, Mark Bergen, Daniel Levy, Mark Ritson, and Mark Zbaracki. "Pricing as a Strategic Capability." *MIT Sloan Management Review* 43 (Spring 2002): i3, p. 61(6).

15. Richard Brandt. "Bill Gates's Vision." *Business Week* (June 24, 1994): p. 57.

16. Susan Greco. "Where Great Ideas Come From." *Inc.* (April 1998): p. 076.

17. Quoted in *Financial Executive* 18 (March 2002): i2, p. 34(8).

18. Holly J.Wagner. "EXIT Strategy: Bank of America slams the revolving door by asking agents how to make their jobs better." *The ICCM Journal* (February 2001).

19. Case study. www.leedstec.org.uk.

## Chapter 3    *The Dilemma of Empowerment*

1. www.capitalone.com.

2. Heini Nuutinen. "Ready for take-off?" *Airfinance Journal* 208 (Jul/Aug 1998): pp. 28–32.

3. Interview with Scott Abbey, October 2001.

4. Debi O'Donovan. "Play by the new rules (Ending paternalistic employment techniques)." *Employee Benefits* (January 2001): p. 26.

5. William B. Moffett. "Outcomes of Teamwork at FMC." *At Work, Stories of Tomorrow's Workplace* (March/April 1994): p. 9.

6. Kristin Gilpatrick. "External focus, internal answers." *Credit Union Management* 23 (August 2000) (8): pp. 15–19.

7. Dr. John Redding and Dr. Richard Kamm. "Involve All Staff in Strategic Planning." *Credit Union Executive* 40 (March 2000): i2, p. 28.

8. Heini Nuutinen. "Ready for take-off?" *Airfinance Journal* 208 (Jul/Aug 1998): pp. 28–32.

9. Philip Siekman. "Seagate's Three-Day Revolution." *Fortune* (February 2001).

10. Suzy Wetlaufer. "Organizing for Empowerment: An Interview with AES's Roger Sant and Dennis Bakke." *Harvard Business Review* 77 (Jan–Feb 1999): i1, p. 111(1).

11. Kathleen D. Dannemiller and Therese Fitzpatrick. "A vision without action is a daydream. Action without a collective vision is a nightmare!" *Organization Development Journal* 20(2) (Summer 2002): pp. 104–109.

12. "P&G Gets the Formula Right." *Financial Express* (October 5, 2001).

13. Ram Charan. "Conquering a Culture of Indecision." *Harvard Business Review* (April 2001).

14. Alan G. Robinson and Sam Stern. *Corporate Creativity: How Innovation and Improvement Actually Happen.* San Francisco: Berrett-Koehler Publishers, 1997: pp. 159–166.

## Chapter 4    *The Power of Improvisation*

1. Rosabeth Moss Kanter. "Strategy as Improvisational Theater: Companies that want to outpace the competition throw out the script and improvise their way to new strategies." *MIT Sloan Management Review* 43 (Winter 2002): i2, p. 76(6).

2. Alan Robinson, Quoted in "Fostering creativity: Companies enhance the bottom line by building corporate cultures that encourage employee innovation," by Liz Simpson. *Training* 38 (December 2001): i12, p. 54(4).

3. Steve McDougall and Jeff Smith. "Wake up Your Product Development." *Marketing Management* (Summer 1999).

4. Ibid.

5. Ibid.

6. Ibid.

7. William G. Lee, "A Conversation with Herb Kelleher." *Organizational Dynamics* (Autumn 1994): p. 70.

8. "Associates keystone to structure." *Chain Store Age* 75(13) (Mid-December 1999): pp. 54–56.

9. "Wal-Mart: Retailer of the Century Supplement." *Discount Store News* (October 1999): pp. 27–28.

10. Jay Akasie. "Learning from mistakes." *Forbes* 159 (April 7, 1997): n7, p. 20(2).

11. John A. Byrne. "Enterprise." *Business Week*, Enterprise Special Issue (1993): p.14.

12. Interview with Robert Silver, October 2001.

13. Robert Kazel. "Fighting the system; Can't do the job? Maybe it's not you." *Chicago Tribune* (July 21, 2002).

14. Susan Greco. "Where Great Ideas Come From." *Inc.* (April 1998): p. 76.

15. Holly Acland. "Harnessing internal innovation: Many companies fail to exploit the best source of ideas available to them—their staff." *Marketing* (July 2000).

16. Jeanie Casison. "Power to the People—Human Resources Forum: Employee Motivation." *Incentive* (June, 2001).

17. Bob Nelson. "Making employee suggestions count." *ABA Banking Journal* 34 (March 2002): i2, p. 12(1).

18. Alison Coleman. "Open to Suggestions." *Director* (July, 2001).

19. Andrew Das. "ABB's funnel project sparks ideas, innovation." *Research Technology Management* 45(3) (May/June 2002): pp. 18–20.

20. "Enjoy the relationship." *Beverage World* 119(1695) (October 15, 2000): pp. 30–38.

21. David Dritsas. "Kenwood's 2001 plan of attack." 43(5) *Dealerscope* (May 2001): p. 12.

22. Anthony W. Ulwick. "Turn Customer Input into Innovation." *Harvard Business Review* (January 2001).

23. American Productivity and Quality Center Best Practice Report. "New Product Development: Gaining and Using Market Insight." 2001.

24. www.compaq.com.

25. www.newsroom.cisco.com (October 4, 2001).

26. Elisabeth Boone. "An insurer that listens." *Rough Notes* 142(7) (Jul 1999): pp. 24–28.

27. Charles R. Weiser. "Best Practice in Customer Relations." *Consumer Policy Review* (July 1994).

28. Polly La Barre. "The Dis-Organization of Oticon," *Industry Week* (July 18, 1994): p. 26.

29. Amar Bhide. "Hustle as Strategy." *Harvard Business Review* (September–October 1986).

## Chapter 5  *Thinking like a Strategist*

1. Quoted in *Harvard Business Review* 77 (Jan–Feb 1999): i1, p. 111(1).
2. Jeanne Meister, "Learning from the CEO." *Corporate Board* 21 (Nov 2000): i125, p. 21.
3. Alan Deutschman. "How HP Continues to Grow and Grow." *Business Week* (May 2, 1994): p. 90.
4. Robin A. Karol, Ross C. Loeser, and Richard H. Tait. "Better New Business Development at Dupont-I." *Research Technology Management* (January/February 2002).
5. Ron Donoho. "Steering new sales." *Sales & Marketing Management* 153(11) (November 2001): pp. 30–35.
6. Tom Murphy. "Intel Attacks Mobile Market On All Fronts." *Electronic News* 47 (October 8, 2001): i41, p. 14.
7. Doris Jones Yang. "Chipping away at the Wintel duopoly (Transmeta microprocessors vs. Intel/Windows)." *U.S. News & World Report* 129 (November 27, 2000): i21, p. 56.
8. Barnaby Feder. "Start Up Chip Maker Lays Off 40% of its Workers," *The New York Times* (July 19, 2002): p. C7.
9. Connie Guglielmo. "Informix—in his dreams." *Upside* 9(7) (July/August 1997): pp. 96–101+.
10. Gene J. Koprowski. "Abandon Chip? For Transmeta, the mystery and the romance are gone." *Ziff Davis Smart Business for the New Economy* (March 1, 2001): p. 46.
11. Daniel Roth. "How to Cut Pay, Lay Off 8,000 People, and Still Have Workers Who Love You: It's easy: Just follow the Agilent Way." *Fortune* 145 (February 4, 2002): i3, p. 62+.
12. Jennifer W. Martineau and Walter W. Tornow. *Issues and Observations* 14, no. 3 (Center for Creative Leadership, 1994): p. 8.
13. *Quality* 41 (January 2002): i1, p.10.

14. Julie Bennett. "A Question of Trust." *Chicago Tribune* (May 5, 2002).
15. *Quality* 41 (January 2002): i1, p.10.
16. Nguyen Quy Huy. "In Praise of Middle Managers." *Harvard Business Review* (May 2001): pp. 73–79.
17. Alex Taylor III. "Nissan's Turnaround Artist: Carlos Ghosn is giving Japan a lesson in how to compete." *Fortune International* 145 (February 18, 2002): i4, p. 34+.
18. David Magee, quoted in Alan Cowell. "N-I-S-S-A-N: Rah! Rah! Rah!" *New York Times* (February 9, 2003).
19. Janice Castro. "When the chips are down." *Time* 144 (December 26, 1994): n26, p. 126(1).
20. David Kirkpatrick. "Intel's tainted Tylenol?" *Fortune* 130 (December 26, 1994): n13, p. 23(2).
21. Alex Taylor III. "Luxury cars: new leaders in an upscale upheaval." *Fortune* 119 (April 10, 1989): n8, p. 66(7).
22. *The Futurist* 28 (July–August 1994): n4, p. 45(1).
23. Bradford. "Creative Teams at Hewlett-Packard." *Management Development Review* (1997).

## Chapter 6    *The Front-Line Strategist*

1. Cited in *The Pryor Report*. 10: 5A, p. 6.
2. Ben Van Houten. "Personnel Perspective." *Restaurant Business* (2001).
3. Robert A. Nozar. "Guests' Input Helps Develop Standards." *Hotel and Motel Management* (May 7, 2001).
4. "Get inside the Lives of Your Customers." *Harvard Business Review* (May 2001).
5. Charles R. Weiser. "Best Practice in Customer Relations." *Consumer Policy Review* (July 1994).

6. Suzy Wetlaufer. "Organizing for Empowerment: An Interview with AES's Roger Sant and Dennis Bakke." *Harvard Business Review* 77 (January-February 1999): i1, p. 111(1).

7. *The Business Journal* (Serving Charlotte and the Metropolitan Area). 16 (September 14, 2001): i24, p. 15.

8. www.unilever.ch.

9. Susan Greco. "Where Great Ideas Come From." *Inc.* (April 1998): p. 076.

10. Francis J. Gouillart and Frederick D. Sturdivant. "Spend a day in the life of your customers." *Harvard Business Review* (January–February 1994): pp. 116–125.

11. Kathleen Melymuka. "Walking With the Users." *Computerworld* (December 7, 1998).

## Chapter 7  *The Strategy Integrator*

1. Interview with Sid Olvet, March 2002.

2. "Why CEOs Fail." *Fortune* (June 21, 1999): p. 68.

3. Nguyen Quy Huy. "In Praise of Middle Managers." *Harvard Business Review* (May 2001): pp. 73–79.

4. Ibid.

5. Ibid.

6. Karl Walinkas. "From Vision to Reality." *Industrial Management* 42 (November 2000): i6.

7. "Core values: employees favor companies that support social issues." *Incentive* (November 2000): p. 7.

8. Stephen Kerr. "On the Folly of Rewarding A While Hoping For B." *Academy of Management Journal* 18: pp. 769–783.

9. Bob Andelman. "More than a Pat on the Back." Corporate Meetings & Incentives (October 1, 2002).

10. Alison Overholt. "In the Hot Seat." *Fast Company* (September 2002): p. 50.

11. Pam Withers. "Finders-Keepers (Tips for attracting and retaining employees)." *CMA Management* 75 (Oct 2001): i7, p. 24.

12. Princeton Research Associates. *Worker Representation and Participation Survey: Report on the Findings* (December, 1994): p. 13.

13. Ibid.

14. Warren Bennis. 21 *On Becoming a Leader*. Quoted in *Pharmaceutical Executive* (July 2001): i7, p. S28.

15. Steven R. Covey, Quoted in "Sacred Space: Leadership." *The Times of India* (June 5, 2000).

16. James Autry. *Life and Work: A Manager's Search for Meaning*. New York: William Morrow, 1994.

17. *The Economist* (US). "A fallen star." (no author given) 334 (March 4, 1995): n7904, p. 19(3).

18. "Lessons from Leeson." www.riskinstitute.ch, 2000.

**Chapter 8   *The Strategic Leader***

1. "Why Companies Fail" cover story. *Fortune* 145 (May 27, 2002): i11, p. 50+.

2. Stephen C. Harper, Paraphrased by Paula Phillips Carson in the *Journal of Leadership Studies* 8 (Spring 2002): i4, p. 103(3).

3. Letter to the Editor. *Harvard Business Review* (January–February 1995): p. 142.

4. James O'Toole and Warren Bennis. "Our Federalist Future: The Leadership Imperative." *California Management Review* (Summer 1992): p. 87. Emphasis in the original.

5. Quoted in *Fortune* (May 16, 1994): p. 18.

6. Donna Shalala, quoted in Joy Lynne McFarland, Larry E. Senn, and John R. Childress, *21st Century Leadership*. New York: Leadership Press, 1993: p. 97.

7. Hedrick L. Smith, quoted in McFarland, Senn, and Childress, *21st Century Leadership*: p. 99.

8. "How you can be a GREAT Leader." *Success* 48 (April 2001): i3.

9. Dale K. DuPont. "Eureka! Tools for Encouraging Employee Suggestions." *HR Magazine* (September 1999): p. 134.

10. "Turning knowledge into action: innovation expert Robert Sutton reveals the mind-set and strategies needed to go from theory to practice" (cover story). *Chief Executive (U.S.)* (August–September 2002): p. SS14(3).

11. Quoted in John H. Sheridan. "Lew Platt: Creating a Culture for Innovation," *Industry Week* (December 19, 1994): p. 26.

12. Milford Prewitt. "Corporate culture: MRG adopts bigger firms' synergistic precepts." *Nation's Restaurant News* 33(32) (August 9, 1999): pp. 82,86.

13. Quoted in Christopher A. Bartlett and Sumatra Ghoshal. "Changing the Role of Top Management: Beyond Strategy to Purpose." *Harvard Business Review* (November–December 1994): p. 84.

14. Quoted Ibid.

15. William W. George. "Mission driven, values centered." *Executive Excellence* 16(8) (August 1999): pp. 6–7.

16. Caroline Louise Cole. "Optimas 2001—Global Outlook: Eight values bring unity to a worldwide company." *Workforce* 80(3) (March 2001): pp. 44–45.

17. James A. Autrey. *Life & Work: A Manager's Search for Meaning*. New York: William Morrow, 1994.

18. Quoted in Jeffrey H. Garten, *The Mind of the CEO*. Perseus Publishing, 2001: p. 146.

19. Lewin, Kurt. "Frontiers in Group Dynamics." *Human Relations* 1: pp. 5–41.

20. Quoted in Michael L. Lovdahl and David H. Gaylin. "Commentary: Strategy Communication." Temple, Barker & Sloane, Inc. Lexington, Mass.

21. Christopher A. Bartlett and Sumantra Ghoshal. "Building competitive advantage through people." *MIT Sloan Management Review* 43 (Winter 2002): i2, p. 34(8).

22. Suzy Wetlaufer. "Organizing for Empowerment: An Interview with AES's Roger Sant and Dennis Bakke." *Harvard Business Review* 77 (January–February 1999): i1, p. 111(1).

## Chapter 9  *The Strategic Organization*

1. Donald F. Kuratko, R. Duane Ireland, and Jeffrey S. Hornsby. "Improving firm performance through entrepreneurial actions: Acordia's corporate entrepreneurship strategy." *Academy of Management Executives*. November 2001.

2. Keith H. Hammonds. "Michael Porter's Big Ideas." *Fast Company* (March 2001).

3. Betsy Weisendanger. "Deming's luster dims at Florida Power & Light." *Journal of Business Strategy* 14 (Sept–Oct 1993): n5, p. 60(2).

4. Mark Henricks. "Quality makes a difference." *Small Business Reports* 17 (December 1992): n12, p. 25(9).

5. David Crisp and Alexandra W. Ballantine. "Oh, baby." *IIE Solutions* (September 2001).

6. Tom Field. "Winner Profile: The Mitre Corp," *CIO* (February 1, 1999).

7. Interview with Jim Bayliss, October 2002.

# Acknowledgments

Writing a book like this is an attempt to convey the experiences and learnings of a lifetime. Those learnings come as a result of the challenge and generosity of others. I thank:

- Evelyn Toynton, without whose brilliance and care this book could not have been written.
- Toni Lucia and Rick Lepsinger, my lifelong partners and friends.
- Anna Ongpin, whose rock-steady professionalism is unfailing and so needed.
- Shannon Rye Wall, many of whose ideas are reflected throughout this book.
- Bill Jockle, my friend and mentor whom I miss dearly.
- Lance Mitchell, Bob Silver, and Tom Waltermire, whose friendship, support and collaboration have helped me help them.
- My many supportive colleagues at Right Management Consultants, including Marc Kaplan, Stan Hubbard, Janet Castricum, Sid Nachman, Terri Lowe, Dalene Foster, Jennifer Forgie, Kelly Fitzgerald, Dennis Taylor, Kim Tamru, Jaime Bruderek, and Andy Mutch.

# ACKNOWLEDGMENTS

- Max Wolf, for his invaluable assistance and research for this project.
- My family: Jack Wall; Alissa, Marc, Samantha, and Dylan Berger; Sandra Wall and Chris, Ethan, and Cameron Walton; Ian, Dana, and Krissy Wall; and Dave Wall, for their love and tireless support.
- And finally, Martina Baginski, who constantly inspires me to see and experience the world in new and exciting ways.

# Index

# INDEX

# Index

# INDEX

# Index

# Index

# About the Author

Stephen J. Wall is Managing Vice President of Right Management Consultants. Steve consults with corporations worldwide on shaping business visions to energize organizational change, emphasizing a flexible and realistic approach to strategy.

In addition to his consulting activities, Steve regularly addresses executive conferences and writes about integrating acquisitions successfully and leading strategically. He is the co-author of *The New Strategists: Creating Leaders at All Levels* and *The Morning After: Making Corporate Mergers Work After the Deal Is Sealed.*